Academic Writing and Grammar for Students

SAGE was founded in 1965 by Sara Miller McCune to support the dissemination of usable knowledge by publishing innovative and high-quality research and teaching content. Today, we publish more than 850 journals, including those of more than 300 learned societies, more than 800 new books per year, and a growing range of library products including archives, data, case studies, reports, and video. SAGE remains majority-owned by our founder, and after Sara's lifetime will become owned by a charitable trust that secures our continued independence.

Los Angeles | London | New Delhi | Singapore | Washington DC

→ **SAGE Study Skills**

Academic Writing and Grammar for Students

2nd Edition

Alex Osmond

Los Angeles | London | New Delhi
Singapore | Washington DC

Los Angeles | London | New Delhi
Singapore | Washington DC

SAGE Publications Ltd
1 Oliver's Yard
55 City Road
London EC1Y 1SP

SAGE Publications Inc.
2455 Teller Road
Thousand Oaks, California 91320

SAGE Publications India Pvt Ltd
B 1/I 1 Mohan Cooperative Industrial Area
Mathura Road
New Delhi 110 044

SAGE Publications Asia-Pacific Pte Ltd
3 Church Street
#10-04 Samsung Hub
Singapore 049483

Editor: Marianne Lagrange
Editorial assistant: Robert Patterson
Production editor: Tom Bedford
Copyeditor: Gemma Marren
Proofreader: Elaine Leek
Marketing manager: Catherine Slinn
Cover design: Stephanie Guyaz
Typeset by: C&M Digitals (P) Ltd, Chennai, India
Printed and bound in Great Britain by Ashford
Colour Press Ltd

Library of Congress Control Number: 2015935649

British Library Cataloguing in Publication data

A catalogue record for this book is available from
the British Library

MIX
Paper from
responsible sources
FSC® C011748

ISBN 978-1-4739-1935-8
ISBN 978-1-4739-1936-5 (pbk)

At SAGE we take sustainability seriously. Most of our products are printed in the UK using FSC papers and boards.
When we print overseas we ensure sustainable papers are used as measured by the Egmont grading system.
We undertake an annual audit to monitor our sustainability.

Contents

About the Author

Photo credit: Maria Wald

Alex Osmond has worked as an Academic Skills Adviser and Project Manager at two UK institutions: Cardiff Metropolitan University and Brunel University. As part of these roles, he has provided guidance to students, both online and face-to-face, focusing on the development of their academic writing. Students have been consistent in praising the advice he has given, which has often translated directly into higher grades. Alex has also taught a wide variety of skills sessions across specific degree programmes. He has worked to develop online resources aimed at improving academic writing, and also co-managed the Study Skills Collection at Brunel University Library. A module that Alex helped devise at Cardiff Metropolitan was nominated for a Times Higher Education Award in Outstanding Student Support. Alex has focused on the English language in his studies and work for several years, and his approach highlights the importance of independent learning in students developing a well-rounded set of skills.

Acknowledgements

Many people were involved in putting this book together, contributing ideas and generally helping me through the daunting experience of writing and publishing a first book. I'll admit that I hope it gets easier, but at the same time, it's been a very positive experience!

The team at SAGE made this experience much less stressful than it could have been, and the feedback, assistance and patience provided by Marianne, Kathryn, Robert, Catherine and Lucia throughout the writing, and the inevitable delays, were invaluable. Gemma Marren also provided thoughtful and enlightening copy-editing.

I'm grateful to all the tutors and lecturers who provided their valuable time, thoughts and quotes. They are, in no particular order: Emily Danvers, head of the Academic Skills team; Dr Fiona Cullen, Youth and Community Work lecturer; Dr Martin Greenhow, lecturer in Maths; Dr Simon Kent, Computing lecturer (whose project management module also helped me a lot with another initiative I became involved in!); Alice MacKenzie, Occupational Therapy tutor; Dr Kelly Ashford, Sports Psychology tutor; Dr Mariann Rand-Weaver, Biosciences lecturer and tireless Pro-Vice Chancellor. I am also grateful to Dr Amélie Gourdon-Kanhukamwe at Kingston University for expanding on her review of the book by providing a useful 'What your tutors say' section.

I received a lot of support from the staff I worked with in the library – in particular, Ann and Lorna deserve a mention. Emily, who I'm proud to mention twice in the list, and Courtney, were wonderful colleagues who continue to make Brunel's Academic Skills service the envy of the sector! I must also mention Sarah Williams at Cardiff Metropolitan, who instilled in me my interest in helping students improve their writing.

My unexpected but never-regretted move – to work with online learning while writing this book – could have disrupted things considerably. Paal Elgvad, having taken me under his wing, made this transition as smooth as possible and he accepted last-minute pleas for days off with almost saintly virtue and good cheer!

My family, of course, provided incredible encouragement. My brothers, Laurence and Conrad, provided drive by reading sections, commenting and lamenting that they didn't have a book like this when they were studying. My mother, Magda, has supported all of us through triumph and tribulation and is the strongest person I know. My father, Jonathan, inspired me to work in academia and I will always look up to him. My friends – Sarah, Eimear and Ellie in particular – put up with my behaviour during the stressful times, and celebrated with me during the better ones.

And, of course, Kate, who was far, far too patient with me – much more than I deserved.

SAGE would like to thank the following reviewers whose valuable feedback helped to shape the new edition:

- David Biggins, Bournemouth University
- Kate Daniels, University of Cambridge
- Ruth Hewston, University of Worcester
- Neil Rutledge, Cumbria Primary Teacher Training.

Introduction

The Aims of this Book and How to Use It

Writing at university

Writing essays and assignments is difficult. I imagine many of my readers agree with that statement. Understanding what is expected of you at university level, and then meeting these high academic standards, are daunting skills. In fact, you'll never be finished: it is always possible to improve your essay-writing skills, and to make your written work more effective.

What is more, writing effective, high-quality assignments *should* be difficult. Being able to write essays on complex topics to a high standard is a skill worth having. Studying at university gives you the perfect opportunity to develop it. Of course, you must also develop these skills to get the marks needed to pass your course!

One of the things that makes this even *more* difficult (apart from the wide range of challenges that come with studying in higher education) is the fact that you are expected to develop these skills while you are studying for your degree: a whole, complex subject.

At university, you're expected to develop in-depth knowledge and analytical skills in fields like, for example, business, computing, creative writing or philosophy, and, *in addition*, the writing skills to express this knowledge effectively.

My experience working in higher education has taught me that most students are eager to spend time developing their writing skills – as well as other academic skills, such as effective presenting, statistics and time management.

Because these skills will be developed while you are studying an academic subject, you want to be sure that this time is spent *wisely*. This is true of *all* time spent on studying.

Take this situation, for example: if you went to see your personal tutor to discuss a part of her most recent lecture, you would want to make the most of the appointment time you had. You would hope to come away with some meaningful, practical advice.

'Meaningful, practical advice' is a phrase that neatly summarises what I hope this book provides. The book's focus is relatively narrow compared with other books about study skills. The spotlight is largely directed at the basic concepts behind the grammar of academic English, and the conventions of academic writing. More advanced chapters discuss specific techniques to make your writing effective.

By keeping this focus clear and strong throughout the book, I hope to: help you develop your essay writing; make it more effective; and make you aware of the common mistakes or issues that can often lead to lost marks (but, with a bit of work, don't have to).

When the book's focus does become slightly wider (the chapters on critical thinking and referencing, for example), the aim is still to provide to-the-point, practical advice that you can quickly apply to your own written work. The techniques discussed in chapters like this are still those that are vital for improving the quality of the sentences and paragraphs on the pages you write.

This book, then, sticks pretty closely to your writing itself – to the phrases, words and paragraphs on the page. You will find a range of books that tackle academic skills more generally. They might talk more about the planning process, about the structure of assignments and, even further from the printed page, how to give presentations or manage your time.

Many of the books that discuss these things are excellent, but to keep my advice practical I have deliberately chosen a focus that I think matches many of the concerns students have while studying, especially early on in their studies.

I won't dwell on definitions for 'essay' and 'assignment', two words I use almost interchangeably. The rules of academic writing apply across all subjects, and although you will be asked to do different things in your assignments, similar things are expected of you. Any piece of written work longer than, say, 250 words is what this book calls an essay or assignment.

Another word I use throughout the book, and one I *do* want to define quickly, is 'argument'.

'Argument' in this sense doesn't mean a specific debate between two or more people around the kitchen table or at the pub! (That said, academia *is* all about debate; debate based on reason, however – not emotion.)

That more common definition of argument actually comes from the classical idea – argument as a process of reasoning: that is, using evidence and logic to reach a conclusion. That sounds exactly like what should be happening in your essays, doesn't it?

In fact, the nature of writing, studying and learning at Western universities borrows much from classical Greek ideas. Using reason to convince your audience (in this case, your readers) of something (in this case, your answer or response to the essay question or assignment brief) is one of these concepts.

'Critical thinking' is another idea, a vital one while studying at university, which is descended from this classical tradition. Critical thinking is a frame of mind in which you analyse your research, don't take anything for granted and look at all sides of other arguments before reaching your own conclusion.

In Western higher education, this frame of mind, or this way of thinking, is the goal. This is opposed to simple memorisation of facts, and using essays to try to prove to the reader that you've done this memorisation. The book does not focus on critical thinking throughout, but there is a chapter that examines this topic, and how to use other sources in our work, in some detail.

In summary, when you read the word 'argument', I mean not just your essay as a whole, but your specific sequence of logical ideas, with their supporting evidence. This should all be written in a way that convinces your reader that your answer to the essay question is a valid, thoughtful one.

The basic idea behind learning in a British university, and what you are ultimately trying to do, is summarised neatly by Martin:

WHAT YOUR TUTORS SAY

'Seek to understand, rather than memorise facts' – Martin, Maths lecturer

In your essays, you are trying to demonstrate that you *understand* the key ideas underpinning your subject, not that you are particularly good at memorising dates, names or places. Chapter 5 on critical thinking looks at specific techniques to help you demonstrate this, but it is a useful idea to have in the back of your mind as you read on.

Because you are trying to demonstrate a complex, high level of thinking, your writing should be *simple* and *clear* – another key theme this book will mention repeatedly!

What's in this book?

Below are summaries of each chapter. Seeing a brief explanation of the topics included in each chapter, and the order they're in, should help make the book's overall direction clear.

After this introduction, you'll read about:

Basic conventions of academic writing

There are certain rules you must follow in academic writing, and some conventions you have to stick to. There are reasons for this, which the chapter will make clear. Before getting stuck into complex grammatical issues, it will be useful to start with some of the rules you *need* to get your head around when writing essays.

Basic grammatical concepts

This chapter outlines some of the basic grammatical rules you should be comfortable with. The aim is not to learn hundreds of grammatical terms or memorise complex definitions. Instead, the focus is on understanding some fundamental rules, explained with examples from academic writing. You can then make sure to follow these rules, and to put the techniques to practical use in your work.

Putting sentences together

Basic grammar doesn't do much good unless you are actually writing whole sentences! This chapter builds on the previous two by looking at constructing effective, grammatically correct academic sentences – applying the rules and conventions you've already learned.

Putting paragraphs together

After discussing how sentences are put together, the next logical step is to look at how to arrange these sentences to make effective, well-written paragraphs. Some of the rules and ideas in this chapter are similar to those in the preceding one; however, there are also plenty of important additional techniques to bear in mind when writing paragraphs. They will be discussed here.

Critical thinking

'Critical thinking' is a broad term that refers to a certain way of thinking about the sources or texts you're reading as part of your studies. For clarity, I've separated the mechanics of referencing from *how* we effectively bring our research into our own writing and our own arguments – which is dealt with in this section.

As such, this chapter is intended to provide a practical introduction to integrating what you read into your own work in an effective, thoughtful and honest way.

Referencing

This chapter is a continuation of the previous one. Referencing your research correctly is a vital part of academic writing. Referencing is the *practical* or *technical* set of steps to show your reader exactly how and where you've used your sources.

Conciseness and clarity

The chapters up to this point have focused on aspects of academic writing that could be called *essential*. It is *essential* that you follow the academic conventions in Chapter 1; to get your sentences right it is *essential* that you apply the grammar rules from Chapter 2.

This chapter provides ideas, rather than rules, to help the development of your own writing and to make it effective *beyond* the essentials.

These key ideas, illustrated with examples, serve as a starting point. The techniques outlined in this chapter help make writing clear (effective and to the point) and concise (using only the necessary words to make an appropriate point). You'll learn that you have various techniques at your disposal. As you develop as a writer, you'll improve at using these techniques appropriately.

Common mistakes and how to deal with them

My experience giving students guidance on their written work has highlighted certain mistakes and issues that appear too commonly in assignments. These mistakes are made by students at all levels of study and ability. This chapter tackles the main ones, with examples and solutions for each.

I hope that you can dip in and out of this chapter and find something to double-check in your own work. Because I've based this chapter on my extensive experience of reading many different kinds of academic writing, I'm confident that it effectively deals with problems and issues that, in most cases, can be avoided quite easily.

Proofreading effectively

This chapter provides guidance on a vital, but often neglected, part of the writing process: proofreading your work. This chapter discusses techniques to help you ensure that your work is ready for submission, and ready for others to read.

Notes on the text and the conventions I follow

The final part of this chapter highlights a few things you need to be aware of as you read this book. It focuses on the conventions and techniques I use in the following chapters.

Different subjects

The examples of academic writing I use come from a range of different academic subjects. I wrote all of them myself, and as such you should not treat them as factual representations of any topic.

Similarly, all the references I use in the examples are made up. Your focus should be on *applying* the ideas that the examples demonstrate. Learn specific *techniques* from the examples and think about using them in your own work. Don't look for actual content in any of my examples.

Most of the actual ideas and themes discussed in this book, and the key points I make, apply to academic writing on any subject. Whether you are studying social care or sports psychology, computer science or creative writing, law or linguistics, physics or physiotherapy (I have taught academic writing sessions to all the subjects I've just named), the principles behind academic writing will be the same.

Referencing

In my example sentences and paragraphs, I use the Harvard referencing system. As you'll discover in Chapter 6, there are many different referencing styles or systems. More detail will be provided on some of them. There are also principles that apply to all referencing styles.

Put simply, Harvard referencing involves including the surnames of the authors of your source material in parentheses (round brackets). These parentheses go inside sentences at appropriate points in your text, along with the year the source material was published.

For the sake of simplicity, I wanted to choose *one* style and stick with it. I use the Harvard style because it is relatively simple and used by many UK universities across a range of subjects. As mentioned above, all the references I use are *fictional* and I use them to demonstrate writing techniques only. In most cases the names of authors I use are fictional.

Key point

It's important that you bear in mind that the writing in this book doesn't *strictly* follow all the conventions of academic writing that I tell you about. This book is not an essay. Additionally, is not an academic text in the same way most of your textbooks are.

To maintain a friendly and accessible tone, there are some techniques I use that you should avoid in your essays.

Because this is such an important fact, I will repeat it at appropriate points throughout the book.

To summarise, however, so you have an idea going forward:

I use the second person 'you' to address my readers throughout the book. As you'll learn in the next chapter, this is not acceptable in academic writing.

Similarly, I use the first person 'I' and 'my' to refer to myself. This is something to avoid in *most essays*. Some subjects involve a kind of writing called 'reflective' writing, in which the author of an essay discusses their own experiences in an academic context. Outside of this particular type of academic writing, however, the first person and references to yourself as the author of a piece of work should not appear.

You should not use 'contractions', in which words are joined together, and letters removed, to be replaced with an apostrophe. For example, 'won't' is the contracted form of 'will not'. I use some contractions to maintain this sense of friendliness that would not be appropriate in an academic essay.

Finally, I use some phrases that could be deemed colloquial; some that might even be considered slang.

Key point

I use 'Key point' boxes like the one you can see above throughout the book. They emphasise certain key ideas or points, or highlight specific examples of a certain technique. Some chapters have several boxes like this, and some of them have only a few.

I don't have any specific rules for each box, and I hope everything I've written is important. However, if I think a certain point should stand out from the rest of the text it'll appear in a box like this.

WHAT YOUR TUTORS SAY

Throughout the book, you'll also see these 'What your tutors say' boxes. Experienced academics who teach a range of subjects (I give the subject with their name) have kindly provided me with their thoughts and tips on many of the things I write about in this book. I only use first names in the text itself, but you can find more information about who they are in the Acknowledgements.

These brief quotations give you the chance to hear from the kinds of people who will actually be marking your work. In most cases, I use the quotes from the lecturers to begin a discussion of my own, or to reinforce a point I am making. This actually parallels the kind of thing you should aim to do when you reference other sources.

Now that I've introduced the topic, let's get on with it!

1

Basic Conventions of Academic Writing

Learning outcomes

By the end of this chapter you should:

- have an awareness of the basic conventions and formal tone of academic writing
- understand why academic writing is written in a certain way
- be able to use some of the basic conventions in your own work.

My aim in this chapter is to highlight the main, basic conventions of academic writing. A 'convention' is, in some cases, a rule to follow, or it can be a technique your tutors expect to see used in your assignments. Your lecturers, professors and other tutors have to follow these same rules when they publish books and journal articles.

If you are used to writing essays, you may find that you are familiar with much of this material, some of which I would consider 'basic'. If you're just starting at university, or haven't studied for a while, some of these ideas might be newer to you.

Read this section carefully. It's surprising how often students submit essays with these conventions ignored or misused. 'How' to write at university is just as important as 'what' to write. The two go together.

> ## WHAT YOUR TUTORS SAY
>
> 'Correct grammar and referencing indicate that you care about how you present yourself' – Mariann, Biosciences lecturer

Mariann makes this same point: your knowledge of a particular subject, and the content of your answer to an essay question, by themselves are not enough to satisfy the tutors marking your work. You are expected to engage with the academic debate in an academic way, and 'present yourself' accordingly. Mariann mentions grammar and referencing; this also applies to academic conventions.

As you progress through your studies, this material will become more familiar. Most of these conventions apply to presentations too. Becoming comfortable with these basic rules is greatly helped by the *reading* we have to do as part of our time at university.

When you read a journal article for your next seminar, or learn how to perform a particular experiment from a textbook, or are simply picking relevant books from the library shelves, don't just focus on the *content*, as important as that is. Try to absorb the way these conventions come up again and again in all the academic writing you'll have to *read*.

It's really important to pay close attention to your reading, beyond its content. This is *the* best way of developing your own writing. Books like this, and the academic skills workshops your university runs, are important; but only if you are doing the reading expected of you, and then *more*. I have already mentioned this, and will continue to repeat this point throughout the book, because it is a vital, overlooked and very *simple* way of slowly developing and improving your own writing.

Why does academic writing have rules? Good academic writing has various qualities: it is clear, formal, objective and supported.

Additionally, because you are writing about potentially complex ideas, it should be as simple as possible, in order to make these ideas clear. So academic writing might end up being complex, but you should never *try* to write things in a complex way. Discuss your ideas at a high enough level, and the complexity is almost like the 'side effect' you get with medicines; it is not an actual objective of your writing. At university, you'll be discussing serious and important ideas a lot of the time, and complexity will naturally grow out of that.

More examples of some other academic techniques appear in the chapter 'Common Mistakes and How to Deal With Them'. In that chapter I also provide more examples of how issues appear and how to resolve them. The aim of this chapter is to *introduce* you to the *basic* conventions. After that, we can look at grammatical issues and the process of actually putting an argument together. This list is not meant to be exhaustive, but I have tried to cover the most important and common conventions.

Before we go on to discuss some conventions one-by-one, it's worth noting one final point. This book does not stick to all of them. I intended to write a friendly, easygoing guide. You already have plenty of reading to do as part of your course. I've explained how important it is that you take the time to learn from that too!

Although my writing is *relatively* formal, the level of formality is occasionally lower than would be expected of your essays – the exclamation mark I used in the previous sentence, for example, and the way I address my readers as 'you', are examples of features in my writing that would not be appropriate in an academic essay. Where this point is particularly important, I'll highlight it again.

Using abbreviations

Abbreviations are words grouped together then referred to by their first letters. You're likely to encounter many in an academic environment. Here are some examples: BBC, HEI, USA, IT.

Key point

You have probably heard the term 'acronym' before; I use 'abbreviation' here. What's the difference? In spoken English, acronyms are actually pronounced as they're written: think about the examples 'NATO' and 'AIDS'. You don't pronounce 'BBC' as written, which would sound awfully strange – you use the letters individually. Many people, however, use the terms to mean the same thing, and in written English you don't need to worry about the difference anyway.

These must be written in a particular way in academic writing. This is an excellent example of a simple convention that, followed properly, makes writing clearer. In a 'normal' length essay (anything less than, say, 8000 words), simply write the term out *in full* and indicate the abbreviation in parentheses afterwards. After this, you can just use the abbreviation. Here's an example:

> ✓ The budget cuts proposed raised doubts among officials at the Ministry of Defence (MoD). A spokesman for the MoD confirmed discussions were ongoing.

After the example sentence, the abbreviation 'MoD' could be used.

If you are writing a longer piece of work, like a dissertation, it might be worth occasionally 'reminding' your readers of a particular abbreviation. You might use the full phrase the first time you use it in each chapter. Another option, particularly if a piece of work contains many different abbreviations, is to have a glossary or appendix that lists them all in one place. Ask your tutor what kind of techniques they would like you to use.

Key point

There are some abbreviations which don't need to be given in full. It is unlikely, for example, that you'll need to write 'United Kingdom' instead of UK, because this is common knowledge. I'd also say the same about 'USA'. If in doubt, however, write the full term first, as I did in the example. You will need to exercise judgement as to which abbreviations won't need to be written in full – but *most* of them will.

Establishing objectivity

'Objectivity' is a quality you need your assignments to have. What does it mean to be objective when you write?

Objectivity refers to a deliberate distance between yourself as a writer and the subject matter of your assignment. Being objective is about creating this distance. Objectivity is established in various ways. I discuss some of these ways separately: for example, avoiding the first and second person (discussed later in the chapter) is a way of establishing objectivity by making your writing seem less 'familiar'.

Some students find it useful to think about the opposite of objectivity – 'subjectivity'. If you are writing in a *subjective* way, you seem very close to your subject. Another way to think about this difference is this: imagine objectivity as being on the outside looking in. Subjectivity is being on the inside looking out.

So, instead of writing about your own experiences, you write about the research and reading you've done. Instead of making points based on your *opinions*, write about the conclusion to which your research has led you. Instead of writing based on a chat, or argument, you had with your friends, use an interview you've conducted with an academic *expert* in the field.

There is an important exception to be aware of. Some subjects at university involve a kind of academic writing called 'reflective writing'. Reflective writing is about your reflections on experiences you've had; they will be experiences relevant to the topic or to your course. Writing a report on a work placement you completed, for example, would involve reflection. Reflective assignments ask you to discuss what you've learned from certain experiences, in the context of the theory you've been taught and the academic texts you've read.

More examples include teaching-based courses: you might be asked to write about your week teaching at a school. If you are undertaking any kind of work placement on, for example, an engineering course, you might be assigned to write a diary or some kind of summary of what you did and what you learned. Similarly, if you complete a group project, writing up the way the group made decisions and worked together (which would clearly include you as a member of the group) might also involve recounting your own experiences.

This section has made clear the importance of being objective. Following and understanding some of the other conventions in this chapter will actually help you achieve objectivity in your academic writing.

Using colloquial language or contractions, for example, makes writing seem subjective. This is because your reader will get the impression that you are less serious (and not thinking in an academic way) about your subject.

The first and second person (words like 'I', 'you', etc.) use very *personal* nouns that decrease the distance between writer and subject. Use the third person to create that distance. *Reference* the work of other academics, researchers and authors to show your engagement with the academic debate on a topic.

Below I provide two examples from an essay about the principles community workers need to be aware of during their work. Each sentence is making a similar, though not identical point. One is obviously *subjective*, with little or no distance between the writer and the topic. By contrast, the second is *objective*, and so has established this distance.

Compare:

> ✗ I would feel really hurt if someone passed on personal information about me without my knowledge.

with:

> ✓ Community workers must follow ethical conventions so as not to undermine trust.

Both make a valid point. The first sentence, however, makes the point in a very personal way. The use of the first person 'I' reinforces the sense that the writer is discussing a situation from *their own* frame of reference. The second sentence takes the key point, about ethical conventions, and makes it in a calm, objective way.

Referencing correctly

This work isn't a complete referencing textbook (the conventions of referencing vary from course to course and university to university), but any guide to academic writing must mention it. This is a brief summary; I go into more detail about referencing in a later chapter.

WHAT YOUR TUTORS SAY

'It is essential that your work provides linkages and examples from appropriate academic sources to evidence and provide scholarly context to your work' – Fiona, Youth and Community Work lecturer

Fiona uses the word 'essential': you will almost always be expected to reference other sources in your work. If you write an essay with no references, you will get very low marks. Think about the journals and books you've been reading on your course. They're likely to be full of references.

There are various other words and techniques associated with referencing. Various referencing styles and systems exist (you might hear about 'citing', 'footnotes', the 'Harvard style', 'numeric referencing', and much more). However, *referencing* as a whole means making it clear when the ideas, concepts, quotations, diagrams, definitions, images or arguments in your work come from elsewhere. 'Elsewhere' might mean other books, conferences, journal articles, online sources, and so on.

This will be discussed later on, but a *crucial* part of writing essays and assignments is engaging with the body of research, writing and discussion on a particular topic or subject. There will be a wide selection of ideas at a subject level, and additional debate and discussion about specific parts of the subject or topics within it.

There will always be debate and discussion on a subject. Studying at university level is a way of entering that debate. This is why you'll be made to read books, research, conduct laboratory experiments, and so on.

Referencing, however you are expected to do it, is how you'll point out that a particular quote, for example, came from a specific page in a specific book; or that a particular painting is very important to the history of art.

In short, almost every essay or assignment you write at university should contain references. Be aware that not every essay question you are assigned will explicitly say 'reference other sources in your answer' (some might do, if there are specific texts that you have to include, for example). This does not mean you won't be expected to engage with your reading material and prove that you have done so in your essay. This is expected of students to such an extent that sometimes it is not even pointed out.

In the chapters on critical thinking and referencing, and the final chapter about common mistakes, referencing *effectively* will be examined more closely. Different referencing styles are outlined: you'll need to double-check which one your tutors want you to use.

It will take a long time before you can remember exactly how to reference a particular source, especially an obscure one. Even your lecturers will sometimes have to look up an example for their own work. Whether or not you can do it from memory, you *will* have to reference properly and consistently.

Avoiding slang/colloquial language

Academic writing is formal. This is commonly accepted by most students. What sometimes is not grasped properly is *why* it is formal. Formality in academic writing doesn't come from deliberately writing difficult, complex sentences, or using complex words where simple ones would serve the same purpose. It comes from making sure that no inappropriate informal language, like slang, is used. This also reinforces the sense of objectivity.

If a writer uses familiar turns of phrase from their everyday colloquial language, the sense of distance from the content might be lost. An assignment written in this way would seem more like an informal, spoken 'chat' about a subject rather than an academic discussion.

Additionally, in most cases, academic writing should be *literal*. This means that words and phrases used should operate according to their actual dictionary definitions. Quite often, slang and colloquial phrases from speech are not literal. Here is an example of a common phrase that is not literal and, as such, would be inappropriate in an essay:

✗ It is widely accepted that election campaigns go the extra mile in their final weeks.

15

The phrase 'go the extra mile' means, in informal English, to make additional effort, to try harder. Taken literally, however, this sentence suggests that staff working on political campaigns travel an additional mile nearer election time! A simple, literal version of the sentence might look like this:

> ✓ It is widely accepted that election campaigns increase their efforts in the final weeks.

So what is slang? What is colloquial language? What are colloquialisms? You have just seen an example.

Although most students are aware that they should not use informal language in essays, it is the definition of 'informal' or 'slang' that is more difficult. Unfortunately, this book can only help to a certain extent, and provide some guidelines.

In the following box are some examples, from essays on various subjects, of sentences that contain one or more colloquial words or phrases. Some of them are obviously informal, and might even make you laugh; others might surprise you. I will provide improved versions afterwards.

> ✗ Saddam Hussein was a bad dude.
>
> ✗ The company, in an attempt to cut costs, fired 5 per cent of the workforce in 2004.
>
> ✗ Most of the research cited here concludes with the question how come only two hearings in Parliament have been held about this issue.
>
> ✗ Analysing the tendency of pop music to borrow from dance-based genres from a postmodern standpoint limits conclusions. The scene has never really focused on that kind of stuff.
>
> ✗ Bradshaw (2009) decides that the conclusion is clear as crystal: sporting activity should be promoted more to kids at a young age.

In the first sentence, 'bad dude' is almost laughably informal. 'Dude' is outright slang, and the word 'bad' is just as informal; even worse, 'bad dude' is a subjective value judgement that does not make a point in an academic way. A better idea would be to give the reader actual evidence as to why the author deems Saddam to have been a 'bad dude':

> ✓ Saddam Hussein, after coming to power, embarked on a totalitarian rule of systematic terror; a rule catalogued by many, over the years (Makiya, 1989; Johnson, 2005; Hitchens, 2007).

The second sentence would be acceptable in an essay, except for one word: the verb 'fired', which is actually a slang term. As you've learned, academic writing should be *literal*. Clearly, terminating employment has nothing to do with fire or flames! Here, then, is an example of a word common in speech, but not suitable for an academic essay. This can be easily corrected by replacing the word:

> ✓ The company, in an attempt to cut costs, terminated the contracts of 5 per cent of the workforce in 2004.

In the third sentence, the informal phrase – one that comes directly from spoken English – is perhaps harder to spot. It is the forming of a question with the words 'how come'. Going back to our idea of literal English, we can see that the phrase 'how come' does not really mean anything.

Think about what the question is really asking. How would someone actually ask the question? 'Why have only two hearings been held?', most likely. I can use this to replace the phrase 'how come':

> ✓ Most of the research cited here concludes by questioning why only two hearings in Parliament have been held about this issue.

The fourth example contains two colloquial words or phrases, both in the second sentence.

First, the word 'stuff' is inappropriate in academic writing. It is not literal, and is also vague and informal – three things you do not want your writing to be described as! The phrase 'kind of stuff' is even vaguer, and makes the problem worse.

It is common to describe a particular fanbase as a 'scene' in speech, but here it should be replaced. Imagine this sentence being read by someone for whom English was not a first language. Slang phrases like this will not have the same meaning for them; another reason we should be literal in our words and phrases.

As you'll learn later in the book, the word 'really' rarely adds anything to academic writing (the same goes for 'very'). It doesn't mean much or give the reader any real information. As such, it adds to the informality of the sentence, and should be removed.

Here, then, is a possible adapted version of the second sentence:

> ✔ Analysing the tendency of pop music to borrow from dance-based genres from a postmodern standpoint limits conclusions. The contemporary fanbase of popular music tends not to focus on concepts like these.

The final problem sentence contains one 'cliché', as well as an instance of informal language. In addition, there is another problem with it. It is a different kind of problem, one that this book discusses later, but I will point it out anyway.

The phrase 'clear as crystal' is a 'cliché'. Clichés are common or stock phrases unique to a particular language, and overused in that language. Most clichés, a long time ago, were interesting ways of describing something, but have been used so often and become so popular that they have lost their original effect.

Most people know them, and they are frequently used in speech. Every language has its own clichéd phrases, almost all of them too informal for academic writing.

Many clichés in the English language are based around describing things in subjective ways, which you should avoid in academic writing. Other examples include 'a diamond in the rough'; 'frightened to death'; 'read between the lines'. You'd never have cause to use many of them in an essay, but there are a few that appear occasionally!

'Clear as crystal' can be replaced with one word; the most obvious and simple choice is shown below.

Another problem expression is 'kids'. Literal English is clear on this: 'kids' are juvenile goats (as people who disapprove of the word 'kids' often point out!). The word should be replaced with the most obvious alternative: children.

The last problem, of a different nature, is the final phrase in the sentence: 'at a young age'.

The word 'children', which replaces 'kids', has a definition: it means people at a young age; thus the phrase 'at a young age' is not needed. All it is doing is repeating an idea established by another word.

If the source writer mentions a *specific* age, or refers to children at primary school (or another specific group), then this should be made clear.

This allows two possible approaches:

> ✔ Bradshaw (2009) decides that the conclusion is clear: sporting activity should be promoted more to children.
> ✔ Bradshaw (2009) decides that the conclusion is clear: sporting activity should be promoted more to children at primary school age.

Everyone has some awareness of slang, and colloquial, informal language that they might use in speech. As the examples have shown, however, such language can be harder to detect than you might think.

In the examples, I deliberately ensured that, apart from the problematic phrases, the sentences were academically appropriate. It is quite easy to find, and to avoid writing, entirely colloquial sentences or paragraphs. The occasional informal phrase is more of a danger.

As you read through your work, ask yourself:

- Does each word or phrase mean what a dictionary says it means?
- Is this phrase commonly heard in speech?
- Would I expect to see this in the textbooks and journals I read as part of my course?
- Would someone not as familiar with English as I am translate this correctly?

Think about that last point: someone using an English dictionary to translate 'clear as crystal', from the last example, would probably wonder why your essay was suddenly referring to jewels!

If any of your answers to these questions leaves you in doubt, take the approach we have just used. Replace the phrases you have concerns about with clear, effective, simple alternatives.

Avoiding emotive language

Avoiding emotive language is a skill similar to avoiding colloquial language. It is hard to define at first, but the more you write, the easier it will become.

Emotive language is not just language that could be described as 'emotional'. More than that, emotive language is used *deliberately* to evoke an emotion in the reader. This is common in some journalism, politics and fiction.

WHAT YOUR TUTORS SAY

'Rather than just arguing that, in your personal and/or professional opinion, young people are demonised by the media, provide examples, and cite scholarly work that further supports your observation. Such an approach will prevent tutors writing "evidence?" repeatedly in the margins of your assignments' – Fiona, Youth and Community Work lecturer

Fiona uses a specific example of a potentially emotive topic from her own area of expertise – the 'demonisation' of young people. She recommends using effective referencing from other sources to make it clear you are not just writing, in a subjective way, about your opinions. As you'll see, this is good advice about a very effective technique.

Academic writing involves making points based on evidence. Clearly, then, you do not want to use emotive language in assignments. You must avoid deliberately appealing to the emotions of your readers. Because you might be writing about a subject that has the potential to affect emotions, or provoke a powerful reaction, this can be difficult.

What *is* emotive language, though? Some words and phrases can be emotive in themselves. Others might be perfectly acceptable in an essay unless used as part of a particular phrase or in an emotive way. This is one of the conventions that you have to think carefully about.

Ultimately, you must use your common sense. Emotive language tends to be subjective, like colloquial language. The more you develop an objective writing style, the more naturally you will avoid emotive language.

Unfortunately, it is impossible to put every word in the dictionary into either a column titled 'emotive' or a column titled 'not emotive'! Below are some words and phrases that I'd argue could probably be considered emotive regardless of the context in which they're used. You should get an idea from this list of the kind of language associated with *emotional* rather than *logical* arguments.

- ✗ horrible
- ✗ disgraceful
- ✗ disgusting
- ✗ incredible
- ✗ magnificent
- ✗ dire
- ✗ tragedy
- ✗ wonderful
- ✗ inflict

Key point

The word 'tragedy', included in the above list, is commonly used in an emotive way in some journalism. However, it would be perfectly appropriate to use the term to refer to a play from the tragic genre (like many of Shakespeare's works). Understanding the vocabulary associated with your subject will help you differentiate between the appropriate and emotive use of certain words or phrases.

Here are some short example sentences, from a range of academic subjects, that could reasonably be described as emotive:

- ✗ Many studies (Hurford, 1982; Ryan, 1990; Jackson and Devon, 2002) reinforce the idea that environmental deregulation in Western states can leave parts of otherwise modern, thriving countries as treacherous, barren wasteland.
- ✗ The creation of the NHS by the wartime government of Britain was a towering, even dizzying, achievement.
- ✗ In the play, after the character's baby is born, the torment and turmoil that the family endures is sickening.
- ✗ Where policies like this have been implemented in secondary schools, the schools have raced up league tables.
- ✗ Recent coverage of women's sport in the UK has, sadly, paid almost no attention whatsoever to athletic ability, instead focusing – in a puerile way – on the appearance of the sportswomen.

Two points are worth noting immediately: emotive language is not only associated with *negative* portrayal of a topic. Language can be used to evoke positive emotions; either way, it is not appropriate in academic writing.

Emily, below, points out a problem with any subjective language – her example word is a positive one:

WHAT YOUR TUTORS SAY

'Be wary of using emotive language in your work. Even a word like "good" is problematic as it is subjective and can't be tested or measured. Good according to whom?' – Emily, Academic Skills lecturer

Second, many of these sentences might be making valid points. The first one, for example, references several studies. Just because a sentence contains emotive language does not mean it is 'wrong' – the point just has to be made in an objective way. See Emily's question: 'good according to whom'?

As you can see, most (though not all) emotive language appears as description. Descriptive words (adjectives and adverbs) are discussed in the next chapter – you'll learn that they don't contribute much to academic writing. In the case of emotive description, they can damage your writing. By avoiding descriptive language and only using it when absolutely necessary, you are reducing the risk of using emotive language.

In one example, however, the verb (action word – see the next chapter) is emotive. This is the verb 'raced' in the fourth example. The author is trying to use a *descriptive* verb that does not just describe an action, but gives a sense of *how* the action occurs. However, in this case, it is exaggerated to the point that it becomes an emotive sentence.

Avoiding exaggeration, and exaggerated description in particular, is the best tactic to avoid emotive language – and this is likely to reduce your use of colloquial language too.

Because these sentences are making points to provoke a strong reaction in the reader, simply rephrasing them is not sufficient. You, as the author, have to decide on the evidence you can use to highlight the conclusion you are going to make. This is why I am not going to provide improved examples of all of the above sentences; so much depends on context.

I will improve one of them, however, to demonstrate the process. Here is the original, analysing the relationship between gender and sport:

> ✗ Recent coverage of women's sport in the UK has, sadly, paid almost no attention whatsoever to athletic ability, instead focusing – in a puerile way – on the appearance of the sportswomen.

First, I'll identify the emotive language in the sentence: the word 'sadly', which might be acceptable if the rest of the sentence did not take such an emotive approach; the word 'whatsoever', which makes the claim seem more exaggerated; and the word 'puerile', which is not supported by any evidence, and seems to be the author's view.

To improve this sentence, I'd recommend the following steps: incorporate evidence into the sentence; find examples of the reactions of others to the coverage being discussed – this will make the writing seem less subjective; remove description that cannot be supported by evidence; and make it clear *why* a situation is 'sad' and must be improved, using a combination of evidence and the author's own conclusions.

The result might be something like this:

> ✓ Recent coverage of women's sport in the UK has not focused enough on the sporting ability of sportswomen, according to a variety of research (Darking, 2009; Christopher and Wilson, 2010; Henderson, 2011). This has generated some fierce reaction; Henderson references an interview in which a female footballer accused commentary of being 'puerile' (2001: 24). The research points to the seriousness of the situation, which, regrettably, impacts negatively on gender relationships in younger people (Howard, 2010); a different approach is needed to change this situation.

The second version still expresses the idea that the situation is bad, and even demonstrates the emotional reactions that some people have shown – without being emotional or emotive itself. The references prove that there is agreement that the situation should change, and that there are far-reaching consequences that will continue if it does not.

Ultimately, emotive language, like colloquial language, tends to be subjective, descriptive and exaggerated. The more you base your ideas in evidence, and demonstrate that you are doing so, the more effective your work will be. If there are powerful emotions involved in a debate, demonstrate this by providing examples of them: but do not display your own, or deliberately try to provoke them in your readers.

Avoiding the first person

The 'first person' is a grammatical term for using the words 'I', 'we', 'us', 'ours', 'my', and so on. In the next section on basic grammar, you'll learn more about different types of words. The examples I've just provided, to show you what the first person consists of, are *pronouns*. They can be singular ('I' and 'me' – just referring to you as a single person) or plural ('ours' and 'us' – you are part of a group, perhaps).

The first person is common in many kinds of writing (especially fiction) and in speech. Academic writing is very different – its aim is not to entertain or inform in a popular way, but to make an argument that engages with the academic discussion on a subject.

In this book, I use both the first person and the second person, which I discuss below. Although my writing here is fairly formal, use of the first person was a *deliberate* decision on my part to make the text seem 'friendlier' (and, indeed, less objective).

Students often ask, 'Can I use the first person in my essays?'. Unfortunately, the answer is more complex than just 'no', but not much more complex. If in doubt, do *not* use the first person. Avoid it completely. Sometimes your tutors, or your course handbook, will explicitly tell you not to write in the first person; this makes things easier for you!

Sometimes, however, you might come across use of the first person in your reading, and sometimes you might need to use it in your writing. Very experienced academic writers sometimes use the first person in various ways. The aim here, however, is to become comfortable with the *basic* conventions of academic writing. As such, we will ignore some of these ways in which the first person can be used for effect, and look at the *main* exception to the rule 'do not use the first person in academic writing'.

The main exception is the 'reflective' writing I have already mentioned.

Reflective writing involves reflection on things that have happened to *you*. You cannot pretend they happened to someone else, so you write about them in the first person. It will usually be clear if your assignment requires this kind of reflection. If you are in doubt, ask your tutor if he or she expects use of the first person (which is usually unavoidable in reflective writing).

Below, Amélie provides an example of how reflective writing, along with use of the first person, works in a particular discipline – in this case, Psychology:

WHAT YOUR TUTORS SAY

'More and more often in Psychology degrees, you will be required to write reflective pieces. The distinction mentioned above about the first person will apply. You will also learn to write lab reports, which are structured like short research papers; your final dissertation will follow the same structure. Lab reports and final dissertation are written following the American Psychological Association's (APA, 2009) conventions for publication; their guide is an essential reference for all Psychology students and researchers. One of these conventions is that research papers *should* be written in the first person, what APA calls the editorial *we*. This is mainly to avoid ambiguity: if I write, "The author conducted a review of the literature ..." in a third-person report, it might be not clear whether I am the author or I am citing someone else. Using the first person in a research paper also allows authors to take ownership of their work. The research process is made of decisions – students and experienced researchers, by writing in the first person, show that they own their methods and interpretations ("We suggest ..." is a common phrase, for example). Your Psychology tutor or dissertation supervisor will be able to guide you further on use of the first person, so make sure you speak to them if you are unsure about anything' – Amélie, Psychology lecturer

The APA guide Amélie refers to is this one (you'll learn about these full references, and how to format them, later in this book):

American Psychological Association (2009) *Publication Manual of the American Psychological Association* (6th edn). Washington, DC: Author.

Avoiding the second person

The *second* person is, as you might have guessed, a way of directly addressing someone else. Second person pronouns include 'you', 'your' and 'yours'. Some languages have a different word for the plural 'you' (several people being addressed directly) and the singular 'you' (just one person), but English does not.

However, the second person in English has a very distinct purpose beyond allowing you to talk or write to people (imagine writing a text or email to a friend without using 'you'!). It is used, quite often, in a *general* way, meaning 'people'. This is very common in spoken English.

I'll give you some examples to show you what I mean:

> ✗ If you want a career in engineering, you will have to show dedication and focus.

Now, if this is a careers adviser speaking to a specific student or group of students, then the second person is entirely appropriate (though it wouldn't be an example of academic writing). However, if you write this in an essay about the engineering industry, you are talking *generally*. Substitute 'people' for 'you' and the sentence means the same thing. Substitute, then, 'people' for the first 'you', and the pronoun 'they' for the second 'you'. Using 'people' twice would result in an odd sentence. This leaves you with:

> ✓ If people want a career in engineering, they will have to show dedication and focus.

Here's an example from an English essay, discussing poetry:

> ✗ You really have to read Donne's poetry aloud to fully appreciate his use of language.

Again, what the student here means by 'you' is 'the reader'. While *you*, reading the essay, might technically be called the reader, it is reasonable to assume the student is not addressing *you*, because he or she is addressing *everyone* reading the assignment.

Unlike the use of the first person, the second person should simply be *completely avoided in all academic writing*. When students use the second person in an essay (this is, unfortunately, a *very* common issue) it is almost always in the general way. This makes writing very informal because it is an aspect of spoken English. Remember, to create objectivity and a sense of academic discussion, things we might *say* as part of a less formal conversation might not be appropriate in academic writing.

It is very easy to check if you have used the second person in a typed assignment. Almost all word processors have a 'find' tool – use it, and search for the word 'you'. It will highlight the word wherever it appears. It will also find 'your' because the first three letters are the same.

Then, simply ask yourself, '*who* do I actually mean?' and make this clear. If you are using it in the general way (which is likely), rephrase the sentence.

Work out what key point you are making and write clearly and simply in the third person.

Take the example from the English essay, above. The sentence is making a basic, and potentially valid, point – that Donne's work is better appreciated, or understood, when read aloud. The sentence can be rewritten in several ways to say that quite clearly, with no use of the second person 'you'. One way of doing this might be:

> ✓ Donne's work is best appreciated when spoken aloud.

An alternative sentence would be:

> ✓ Reading Donne's work aloud gives the reader a better sense of the poems.

Both are simple and clear and make the same point without using the second person. The important thing here is not to think too hard about how to remove the 'you'; just do it *as simply as you can*.

Here is another example:

> ✗ The financial crisis in 2008 showed that sometimes you can't rely on the opinions of experts because nobody predicted the crisis.

'You' is being used in the general way. The basic point of the sentence can easily be expressed without 'you'; here is just one possibility:

> ✓ Most experts failed to predict the financial crisis in 2008, which highlights the problem of relying on expert opinion.

There is another important rule to remember when resolving this problem. Students, finding they've used the second person 'you', sometimes think it's appropriate to replace it with the first person 'we' instead.

This is not common in speech, but for some reason is intended to serve a similar purpose to 'you' in essays. I'm not sure why students do this, but I have read it so many times I wanted to warn you here *not* to simply replace the second person 'you' with 'we'. For example:

Do *not* change:

> ✘ You can't understand the conflict between Russia and Georgia in 2008 without an awareness of the region's history.

to:

> ✘ We can't understand the conflict between Russia and Georgia in 2008 without an awareness of the region's history.

but instead to something like:

> ✓ An awareness of the region's history is needed to understand the conflict between Russia and Georgia in 2008.

In short: do not use the second person, and when removing it, do not simply replace it with the first person. Use the more objective third person instead.

Avoiding contractions

A 'contraction' is one word made up of two or more words that have been joined together. Some letters from the words are left out and replaced with an apostrophe.

The apostrophe is a piece of punctuation that is misused in many ways. Some of these are discussed in Chapter 2 on basic grammar and in Chapter 8 on common mistakes. Here, I focus exclusively on contractions – specifically, *not* using them in academic writing. This is another convention I have *not* rigidly followed in this book.

Examples are not hard to find, particularly in speech or popular writing:

- 'cannot' in its contracted form is 'can't'
- 'will not' becomes 'won't'
- 'he is' or 'he has' become 'he's'
- 'should not' becomes 'shouldn't'
- 'there will' becomes 'there'll'.

The rule is simple: do not use contractions in academic writing.

Luckily, as with some of the other conventions, contractions are quite easy to find during your proofreading process. Just type an apostrophe into the 'find' tool of your word processor and you can examine the apostrophes you have used, one-by-one.

This will, of course, mean checking apostrophes used for other reasons (like possessives, or when quoting other sources; both will be mentioned later in the book). However, as soon as you see an apostrophe used in a contraction, you can just type the words out in full. It is certainly not worth losing marks because of an issue so easily fixed.

Simplicity, clarity and conciseness

This is not a single convention, but a broader issue of writing style. The example discussed below is longer than the previous examples in this chapter, and it involves more complex issues.

The later chapter called, unsurprisingly, 'Conciseness and Clarity', looks in more detail at specific techniques to make your writing effective. However, the sooner you start thinking about this issue, the better you will be at putting it into practice.

The three ideas are so intertwined I will not separate them. Essentially, you should use as few words as possible to make a point (conciseness); these *individual* words should be as straightforward as they can be without being informal or inappropriate (simplicity); and they should be put together in a way that makes your point effective and easy to understand (clarity).

This is a key theme of the book in a way that the other subsections of this chapter are not (this book is not, for example, all about abbreviations). Writing simply, concisely and clearly is, however, a key *convention* of academic writing.

In fact, it is a key theme of the book *because* it is an essential convention of academic writing.

For now, I'm going to take one example and discuss it in some detail. In the same way that many of these conventions reinforce objectivity in writing, many also reinforce *clarity*. Conciseness is a feature of our writing that we have to learn to perfect ourselves. It is difficult!

Take a look at the two extracts below. Then you can read my explanation of the changes.

✗ To succeed in obtaining and achieving the highest possible marks in assignments, students must engage in a genuine and concerted attempt to conduct extensive research, devote much time to the planning process, and finally ensure they are entirely comfortable and confident with the rules of English grammar.

✓ To receive the highest possible marks in assignments, students must research effectively, spend enough time planning, and make sure they are confident with grammar.

Would you agree that the two extracts say very similar things? I'd argue that they say practically identical things. The first is over-the-top, unnecessarily formal and repetitive, and overlong. We do not need to labour our points. The second is clearly much shorter, which will give you valuable space to make more points, or support this one with references.

What follows is an outline of my thought process and reasoning behind the changes I've made; as you can see, I've rephrased/reworded large parts of the first version, as well as deleting sections. Everyone will do this kind of thing differently, and there are many different ways I could have altered the first example. So rather than seeing my explanation as a 'solution' to a specific problem, try to see it as an example of one approach to the convention of writing clearly and concisely. Try to view it, also, as showing you the kind of state of mind you should be in when you edit what you've written.

This following section is quite detailed. You might need to return to this part of the book. For now, read over this a few times – you'll see how many techniques and approaches to writing there are, and how many choices you have to make. The more you read, and the more you write and adopt these conventions, the more naturally you will think about the following kinds of points.

With all that in mind, let's take a look at why I changed the extract.

To begin with, the sentence is too long. Even if I hadn't managed to shorten it as much as I have, I would have broken it down into several shorter sentences. Read it aloud and you will probably end up breathless. This is a sure sign a sentence is too long. Sentences that make you breathless are also likely to be too complex.

I thought that 'To succeed in obtaining and achieving the highest possible marks' could be reduced to 'to get the highest possible marks'. Surely using the verbs 'obtaining' *and* 'achieving' is unnecessary. These two words are doing the same thing in the sentence. The student is doing the same thing with the marks – receiving them.

I *could* have used the verb 'to get', but 'get' can often seem informal. 'Get' can be a troublesome verb. Many languages that are similar to English do not have a direct equivalent.

Key point

Here is another quick example that illustrates potential problems with the word 'get'. Compare 'the patient got better' and 'the patient recovered'. The second is more formal, and shorter too.

Moving on, I've shortened 'students must engage in a genuine and concerted attempt to conduct extensive research'. In the second sentence I replace this with 'students must research effectively'.

Ask yourself: if you go into the library, eager to write your best essay yet, and you 'engage in a genuine and concerted attempt to conduct extensive research', what are you actually doing? You are researching *well*. That wasn't formal enough, so I went with *effectively*, which means a similar thing. You are researching in a way that provides you with lots of great points to go into your essay. I could also have used 'thoroughly'.

Key point

The other difference here, which this book discusses further later on, is that I have used a stronger verb. 'Research', a key academic concept, is used as a verb, an action word – 'to research'. In the original, 'research' was a noun. There were two verbs – 'engage' and 'conduct'. Neither means anything without the nouns 'attempt' and 'research' attached to them.

It is better to use effective, strong verbs. Again, think of the difference between 'I conduct research into endangered animals' and 'I research endangered animals'. The verb in the second sentence is stronger, carries more meaning on its own, and because of this the sentence is shorter without losing any of its message.

My updated version of the first extract is certainly not the best or only reworking possible. I could have written, 'students must research extensively and effectively', but I decided that if you are researching effectively, your research is probably extensive too.

My second version has, perhaps, lost the sense of a student trying hard. This can be seen in the first version in the phrase 'a genuine and concerted attempt'. To emphasise that idea of *trying* as well as 'effectiveness', I might write the sentence differently. An example might be: 'students must make the effort to research effectively'.

Next, I changed 'devote much time to the planning process' to 'spend enough time planning'. I thought 'devote' sounded a bit over-the-top, while 'spending' time is perfectly fine. That said, I have, as above, perhaps lost the sense of intense effort.

My worry, though, was that the first extract was not only unnecessarily formal, but seemed too hyperbolic. 'Hyperbole' means deliberately writing or speaking with exaggeration to have a specific effect. This is a technique commonly used in political speeches or opinion-writing. Academic writing should make arguments reinforced by evidence, research and reason.

You'll notice that I also removed the word 'much' from 'much time planning'. The phrases 'a lot of' or 'lots of' are often too vague and informal for academic writing. So you might find yourself writing 'much' or 'many' most of the time instead.

Here though, the word 'enough' is better, because it is more specific. Spending 'much' time is great, but how much is 'much'? A student needs to do the *right* amount of planning. That is, *enough* planning to form the structure of their work. Using 'enough' makes the meaning of the phrase clearer.

Is 'the planning process' all that different from just 'planning'? I'd argue that there is no difference. The 'planning' put into an assignment will include some specific processes. Because of this I used the simpler 'planning' and not 'the planning process'.

I also managed to considerably shorten the last phrase – 'finally ensure they are entirely comfortable and confident with the rules of English grammar'.

I removed the word 'finally' because the reader has come to the last point in the sentence – they *know* it is the 'final' point. My reader will see that a new paragraph begins after this sentence. They will understand from this that the subject is changing, or that I am making a different point. For these reasons I do not think it is necessary to label this 'finally'.

I replaced the verb 'ensure' with 'make sure'. I did not *have* to do this. Making this change has actually turned one word into two; as such, it has not made my work more concise. However, 'ensure' sounded a little too forced and formal to me. I don't think it makes a huge difference, but this is the approach I chose to take. Readers might disagree with me, and the sentence certainly makes sense without this change being made.

This in particular demonstrates quite effectively how writing is about making *choices* as an author. There are certain conventions to follow, but you will always have ultimate control over what goes onto the page.

I made a change to the last part of the sentence. I replaced 'entirely comfortable and confident with the rules of English grammar' with 'confident with grammar'. I removed 'entirely comfortable and confident' simply because I don't think this is true. Not many people ever become 'entirely' confident with English grammar, whether they are studying at university or not.

In fact, a key aim of this book is to help you develop an understanding of the *main* and most important aspects of grammar; the ones you need to write a decent essay or assignment. A fully comprehensive awareness of grammar is not necessary to do this.

Using both 'comfortable' *and* 'confident' is not necessary. It is likely that someone comfortable with a set of rules is confident with them too. There is no benefit, I'd argue, in using both words. I preferred confident, so left that in the sentence.

I removed the word 'English' from 'English grammar'. By getting rid of the reference to a specific language, I made the sentence more versatile. Its key point is broader and more accessible. Surely a writer should be confident with the grammar of whatever language they are working in?

This might seem like a great deal of work to go through to change a short paragraph. In reality, editing the paragraph won't take long – especially as you get used to thinking like this. You'll realise just how quickly you can make meaningful, effective adjustments to your work. One of the aims of this book is to help you develop your skills in this area.

Further reading

Copus, J. (2009) *Brilliant Writing Tips for Students*. Basingstoke: Palgrave.

- This is a short, pocket-sized book that covers key elements of academic style in an accessible, practical way. It includes visual aids to memory that are very useful, as well as examples from actual essays written by students.

2

Basic Grammatical Concepts

Learning outcomes

By the end of this chapter you should:

- understand the definitions of different word types, specifically nouns, verbs, pronouns, articles, modifiers, adjectives, adverbs, conjunctions and prepositions
- have an awareness of how to use these different word types effectively in academic writing
- understand why some grammatical concepts, like modifiers, are less common in academic writing than other types of writing.

This chapter focuses on some key grammatical concepts. These are the grammatical terms and ideas that are most important to ensure your writing is correct and effective.

Because the aim here is to provide practical advice, there is less detail than you might find in books that discuss English grammar as a topic in itself. Similarly, some grammar books are designed to help people learning English as a foreign language. These go into more detail about complex grammatical concepts. At the end of this chapter, you'll find some books that focus on English grammar more specifically, with exercises and tests to complete.

In this chapter, however, the aim is not for you to learn the names of every type of word there is. Nor do you need to memorise or understand some of grammar's more complex ideas.

Having a basic understanding of the key ideas in this chapter should suffice for now. As well as a definition for each key idea, there is a section on effective use. Reading these sections and applying them to your work should ensure that this chapter has a direct impact on your writing.

The next chapter then moves beyond individual word types to examine how sentences are put together in effective, grammatically correct ways.

Before looking at the individual grammatical terms, take some encouragement from the following advice:

WHAT YOUR TUTORS SAY

'To improve your writing, you need to write a lot' – Simon, Computing lecturer

Grammar, sometimes just by reputation, can seem like a difficult, daunting subject. Remembering what Simon points out here can help you feel more positive about this!

Whether or not you memorise grammatical terms, or decide to research further into different types of nouns and verbs, the grammar in your writing will improve *the more you write*. This doesn't just apply to your grammar, of course; all aspects of your writing improve as writing becomes more natural to you.

Your writing will only improve if you *keep* writing, so as you begin studying this tricky subject, try to view each assignment as an opportunity to practise. Even better, the feedback from your tutors for each 'practice' will help you develop even more as a writer.

Types of words

Nouns, concrete nouns, abstract nouns, proper nouns and plurals

Nouns are naming words. They provide names or labels for 'things'. (You'll learn that verbs, on the other hand, are actions.) Every sentence in an essay will have one or more nouns in it (unless they are replaced by pronouns).

Concrete nouns

Concrete nouns are tangible, real things – things you could touch, see or be part of. The clue is in the word 'concrete'.

Examples of concrete nouns you might find in academic writing include:

essay

meeting (this can also be a verb, but here I mean a collection of people in a room – 'a meeting' or 'the meeting')

experiment

therapist

equation

library

Abstract nouns

Abstract nouns are nouns that do not refer to tangible things. Abstract nouns are still names, but you cannot touch or see an abstract noun. Abstract nouns are very common in academic writing, which often directly focuses on abstract concepts and ideas. Here are some examples:

conclusion

intelligence

fear

extravagance

method

Proper nouns

Proper nouns are the names for unique things: specific people, places, brands, companies, and so on. In English, proper nouns begin with a capital letter. Otherwise, they function in sentences as other nouns do. Academic writing involves debate and discussion around existing research; as such, names of authors, experts, researchers and committees, as well as the names of the texts they've written, tend to be mentioned frequently. These are all proper nouns. (The opposite of a proper noun – and so, the name for most nouns – is a 'common' noun.)

Similarly, though it will vary by subject, the names of places, specific events, brands, companies and organisations will often appear. Take a moment to think about the kinds of proper nouns likely to come up in your subject.

Sometimes historical events or academic theories can become proper nouns. As you read in preparation for your assignments, look for the examples from your subject where this has happened. Proper nouns work the same way as other nouns do in sentences; the capital letter is the difference. Here are some examples:

Dr Hofmann

Karl Marx

Toyota

World War II

London

Mount Everest

Key point

Most proper nouns are easy to identify. In academic writing, however, there are often certain nouns associated with certain subjects that have become proper nouns – I've mentioned this above. The best sources of information around this are the things you read as part of your studying. You will get used to using 'Marxism' as a proper noun, and history students will discover many more historical events beyond 'World War II' that are treated as proper nouns.

There are even examples of words that mean one thing when they take a capital letter, and a different thing when they are a normal, as in common, noun. For example, 'Fascism', as a proper noun, refers specifically to the Italian political movement from the 1930s, as practised by the Italian Fascist Party under Mussolini; while 'fascism', the common noun, refers to the broader set of far-right political ideologies. Ask your tutors if you are ever in doubt.

WHAT YOUR TUTORS SAY

'Don't overuse capital letters: "the king, the government, and the parliament"; but, "the reign of King Henry VIII, the National Government of 1931, and the Long Parliament"' – Jonathan, History lecturer

Sticking with history, Jonathan provides some specific examples of common nouns that do not need capital letters, which sometimes become proper nouns because they describe a unique, particular thing. It is very tempting to use capital letters for nouns that are simply associated with or used often in the subject we are studying.

As you research, look at where capital letters are used by other academics. Only use them when you have to.

Plurals

Nouns that refer to multiple things are 'plurals'. In most cases, English nouns become plurals when either 's' or 'es' is added to the end of the word: for example, one 'deadline' is a singular noun; unfortunately, you might need to learn to manage your work when you have multiple 'deadlines' – the plural.

Some nouns are irregular and form plurals differently. Nouns ending in 'y' form plurals ending in 'ies'. Table 2.1 gives some examples.

TABLE 2.1

singular	plural
story	stories
agency	agencies
army	armies
supply	supplies

Nouns ending in 'is' become plurals ending in 'es'. This phenomenon is quite rare, but the nouns do appear in academic writing:

thesis = theses

Some nouns exist in English that do not follow the usual rules when forming plurals; these are known as irregular plurals. The plural of 'index' is 'indices', but there are other nouns ending in 'ex' that form normal plurals ('sex', for example).

It is important to remember that the verbs you use must 'agree' (that is, take the correct form) for the noun or nouns you are using. Some nouns are singular, but refer to a collection of multiple things. Sometimes this results in mistakes in essays.

Key point

Some words you might think are singular are actually plurals, so be careful. The word 'data' (the singular is datum) is a plural, and so is the word 'media' (the singular is medium). Make sure you double-check whether words ending in 'a' are plural or singular. Another example is the word 'criteria', which in the singular is 'criterion'.

Think about, for example, the noun 'group'. Group is a singular noun, even though a group will have several members. The same applies to 'community' or 'organisation'. Remember to double-check whether your noun itself is plural or singular, and make sure you use the correct form of the verb.

The following two sentences would be incorrect:

✗ The group are committed to raising awareness of human rights violations in Burma.

✗ Members of the group is committed to raising awareness of human rights violations in Burma.

The mistake made in the first sentence is surprisingly common. When you proofread, make sure your verbs agree with your nouns. The same applies to pronouns; this is discussed later in the chapter.

The correct versions would be:

✓ The group is committed to raising awareness of human rights violations in Burma.

✓ Members of the group are committed to raising awareness of human rights violations in Burma.

Effective noun use

Beyond making sure that you get the grammatical rules around nouns correct (capital letters for proper nouns and correct use of plurals – errors with these are easy to fix), the main issue around using nouns is to make sure that you use nouns that are specific and simple.

Nouns offer an area where you can demonstrate a varied vocabulary; at the same time, however, you do not want to go to extremes in using odd nouns just to avoid repetition.

Nouns are most effective when there is no alternative word type: in academic writing, especially, where abstract nouns are commonly discussed, sentences can contain large numbers of nouns. This can make writing seem very formal. A balanced mixture of nouns and verbs – which are, as you'll learn, action words – works well.

The following extract, for example, features several nouns that come from verbs. Using the verbs would make the sentence more effective and give it more impact. In the 'common mistakes' chapter, this issue, called 'nominalisation', is discussed in more detail. This essay is about the management of a small business:

> ✗ The day-to-day operating of the business is conducted under the oversight of a small team. Although employee morale is reasonable, a recent review of operations conducted by the executive group found inefficiencies in the small team's planning.

These points can be expressed in a more simple, direct way by replacing some of the nouns with verbs. Here, 'operating' is being used as a noun. 'Oversight' is a noun that also comes from a verb: to oversee. Additionally, 'review' can be a noun or verb; here it is a noun. Finally, 'planning' is a noun here.

A better example might be:

> ✓ A small team oversees how the business operates on a day-to-day basis. Although employee morale is reasonable, the executive group recently reviewed operations and found the small team was planning inefficiently.

Favouring verbs over nouns has made for a clearer extract; it has also allowed me to rearrange some of the sentences to be simpler.

Most subject-specific terms will be nouns. There is a difference between excessive use of complex, formal jargon and appropriate use of nouns associated with the topic your work discusses.

Verbs

Verbs are 'doing' words or 'action' words. Rather than naming things, verbs tell us what is *happening* within a sentence. Put simply, sentences usually consist of nouns carrying out various actions (verbs) to, with or at other nouns.

There are many different kinds of verbs (if you are interested in following them up, look up 'intransitive' verbs, 'transitive' verbs, 'regular' verbs or 'auxiliary' verbs; you'll soon find many other kinds!). Understanding the differences between them, however, is not vital to write assignments simply and effectively.

Here are some examples of verbs written in their 'infinitive' forms. This is a grammatical term that simply means the verb is prefixed by the word 'to'.

---

to write

to investigate

to study

to examine

to develop

to emphasise

to conclude

to undermine

Unlike nouns (except for plurals) verbs change depending on the context they're being used in. Grammar books written in many different languages often demonstrate how to 'conjugate' a verb correctly – that is, put it in the correct form for the appropriate noun – with a layout like the one in Table 2.2. I have taken the verb 'to examine' as my example. This list only covers the *present* tense; the next chapter discusses the *tense* of a verb in more detail.

TABLE 2.2

Infinitive:	To examine
First person singular:	I examine
Second person singular:	You examine
Third person singular:	He/she/it examines
First person plural:	We examine
Second person plural:	You examine
Third person plural:	They examine

Both the 'second person singular' and the 'second person plural' are included for the sake of completeness. Verbs in the English language do not change if the second person is being used to address one person or a group – both are 'you', and the verb form is the same. This is often included in verb conjugation information because some languages do differentiate between the two.

Table 2.3 gives another example of verb conjugation, but for the *past* tense. The verb is 'to conclude'.

TABLE 2.3

Infinitive:	To conclude
First person singular:	I concluded
Second person singular:	You concluded
Third person singular:	He/she/it concluded
First person plural:	We concluded
Second person plural:	You concluded
Third person plural:	They concluded

You'll notice how simple the English past tense seems there. Unfortunately, many of our verbs are irregular and do very different things – try to do the same with the verb 'to write', for example!

In any case, verbs are where the action happens. As you'll find out later, the tense of a verb tells us when the action happens. Together, verbs and nouns make up a great deal of the writing you will do.

Effective verb use

Sentences with clear, powerful verbs often read effectively. This is because verbs, by their very nature, evoke a sense of action, of things happening. They tend to be less formal than nouns.

Like nouns, verbs work best when used specifically. The English language has a wide range of verbs that mean very specific things, or provide a different sense of a similar idea; think of the difference, for example, between 'grow' and 'develop'.

Use simple, clear, effective verbs. Sentences that contain effective verbs give a clear, powerful sense of action. Vary your verbs where possible, but again, don't go overboard.

Key point

Remember that 'to be' is a verb. It is a common verb in many kinds of writing, and in speech – but it is *especially* common in academic writing. Academic writing tends to focus on abstract concepts and ideas more than other types of writing. When ideas are being discussed, the verb 'to be' tends to come up frequently. You will often write sentences containing words like 'is', 'are', 'will be', 'was', 'have been' (all forms of the verb 'to be').

Verbs must 'agree' with the nouns that are carrying them out. In the examples given over the last few pages, you've seen that verbs take different forms for plural nouns. Obviously, the agreement of verbs must remain *consistent* throughout a sentence.

In this example, due perhaps to sloppy proofreading, one of the two verbs doesn't agree with the noun 'committees':

> ✗ These committees attempt to promote diplomacy and raises the profile of charitable groups around the world.

Because both 'attempt' and 'raise' are verbs being carried out by the same noun, they should agree in the same way:

> ✓ These committees attempt to promote diplomacy and raise the profile of charitable groups around the world.

If another noun is introduced, double-check that each verb agrees with the noun carrying out that action.

Some other issues to consider include: avoid using the verb 'get'. It tends to be vague and informal; many other languages do not have the equivalent of such a vague verb. 'Get' is often paired with another word or phrase, but you can usually find a single, more effective verb to replace this.

Some example replacement phrases for verb phrases including 'get' are shown below (there are many others, but this demonstrates the idea):

get bigger = grow

get away from = escape

get better = improve

get worse = worsen/deteriorate

get closer = approach

get less important = diminish

As you can see, an informal phrase like 'get less important' reads much more effectively as 'diminish'. In cases where you can't replace a 'get' phrase, 'become' is often a suitable replacement.

This idea can be applied in another situation: where the verb in your sentence is made up of several words, it is known as a 'verb phrase'. In many cases, these are necessary and appropriate; the problem described in the examples above was that verb phrases including the word 'get' are made informal by the informal nature of that verb.

However, *if possible*, replacing a verb phrase with a single verb is a way of making your verbs more powerful and effective. Replace a verb phrase with one verb if there is a verb that means the same thing; and the single verb is itself appropriate, simple and clear.

Do not spend too much time on this exercise while writing early drafts; in a way, it is a more 'advanced' technique that will improve as you practise. Here are a few pairs of sentences; the first in each contains a verb phrase (in **bold**), and the second a single verb replacement for the verb phrase (also in **bold**):

✗ A common theme in Robertson's later novels is the idea of characters **chasing after** people who abandoned them in the past.

✓ A common theme in Robertson's later novels is the idea of characters **pursuing** people who abandoned them in the past.

✗ The programme of treatment the GP has **told the patient to take** seems **not to deal with** potential psychological problems from the injuries.

✓ The programme of treatment the GP has **recommended to the patient** seems **to ignore** potential psychological problems from the injuries.

✗ In the 'methodology' section, Reese does not **provide reasons for** his decision to conduct a qualitative study.

✓ In the 'methodology' section, Reese does not **justify** his decision to conduct a qualitative study.

These examples demonstrate that, while the use of verb phrases is often appropriate (if sometimes bordering on informal), using single verbs makes a sentence clearer and more effective. Remember that verbs are where the action happens, literally!

In the last example, for instance, the phrase 'provide reasons for' includes a verb ('provide'), a noun ('reasons') and a preposition ('for'). 'Justify' is one verb that replaces all of this. Another possibility might be 'explain': it is up to you as the writer to decide which potential replacement words fit best, depending on what you mean.

In the following, final example, two alternative replacement verbs give the sentence a slightly different meaning. First, read the original sentence, with its verb phrase in **bold**:

> ✗ Several recent news reports (*The Times*, 2010; *The Observer*, 2011) have highlighted how much time MPs **take up** travelling.

Two possible replacements for 'to take up', in the sense of 'time', are: 'to spend' and 'to waste'. It might depend on the nature of the news reports that the essay references, but the sense of these two sentences is very different:

> ✓ Several recent news reports (*The Times*, 2010; *The Observer*, 2011) have highlighted how much time MPs **spend** travelling.
>
> ✓ Several recent news reports (*The Times*, 2010; *The Observer*, 2011) have highlighted how much time MPs **waste** travelling.

The second sentence clearly expresses a negative view, suggesting time spent travelling by MPs could be better spent doing something else. The first, however, is more neutral. Depending on the rest of the paragraph, it might even be expressing a *positive* view – suggesting that the stressful nature of the job, including extensive travelling, means MPs should be respected.

Finally, the 'tense' of a verb – the form a verb takes depending on *when* the action happens – is also an important consideration. Because it affects a whole sentence, however, this is discussed in the next chapter.

Pronouns

Pronouns are used in place of nouns. Again, there are various kinds (demonstrative pronouns, indefinite pronouns, interrogative pronouns, and more) and again, being able to define each kind is not vital to write good essays.

They are very common in all kinds of writing, and in speech.

If you had to refer to 'the author of the study' twenty times on one page, or you were writing an essay about Sigmund Freud and so referred to him throughout an essay, or needed to keep mentioning a particular political ideology like 'neoliberalism', and used these names or nouns in full, your writing would be incredibly long-winded and difficult to read.

The same goes for any kind of writing, and for speech. Once you've made it clear to the reader what you're talking about, or what noun is being discussed at a particular point in your work, you can use pronouns. Here are the most common:

I
you
he
she
it
we

The following words are technically different types of pronouns, but are still used to refer to a particular noun:

which
that
this
these
those
his/hers/its
many
both

Note that pronouns, with the exception of 'I', do not begin with capital letters even if they are replacing proper nouns; unless they are starting a sentence, as usual.

Here is a paragraph with no pronouns: the noun is used in every case. It is obvious how often pronouns are needed, in writing and in speech.

> ✗ The problem with Johnson's study is that at no point in the study does Johnson address any of the criticisms made by other authors of similar studies. Johnson's study, in fact, repeats many of the mistakes found in recent research in this area, and Johnson's conclusions are therefore doubtful. However, some of Johnson's conclusions in Johnson's study do support common themes in research from around 20 years ago (Deckard, 1982; Ribauld, 1984).

Clearly, this is a confusing paragraph. Nearly every noun is repeated. Here is the same paragraph, with pronouns – and other techniques to repeat nouns – used appropriately:

> ✓ The problem with Johnson's study is that at no point in it does Johnson address any of the criticisms made by other authors of similar studies. The study, in fact, repeats many of the mistakes found in recent research in this area, and his conclusions are therefore doubtful. However, some of Johnson's conclusions in the study do support common themes in research from around 20 years ago (Deckard, 1982; Ribauld, 1984).

Note that I did not use a pronoun every time I could have. In the next section, you'll see how important it is to make sure pronouns are used sparingly and clearly.

Effective pronoun use

Because nouns are very common in academic writing, pronouns are commonly needed to refer to them.

Do not overuse pronouns. It is better to repeat a noun if this will avoid confusing your reader. If you are in doubt as to whether a reader will understand what your pronoun means, then use a noun instead. Keep the distance between nouns and their associated pronouns as short as possible.

Always make sure that it is clear which noun a pronoun is replacing. This paragraph contains several pronouns; most of them are potentially confusing:

> ✗ Project management as a field, and area of expertise and research, suffered in the 1970s as it lost standing in the eyes of the public, which witnessed several high-profile projects fail. These were mostly situated in the public sector; this was compounded because at this time it was suffering from a poor reputation anyway. It only began to improve after the introduction of new methodologies and more positive stories in the news. Some of them are still prominent today and organisations in the field work very hard to promote efficient project management; they seem to be enjoying some success.

Most readers would make some sense of the paragraph above, and the general theme is fairly clear. 'Some sense' and 'fairly clear' are not good enough in academic writing, however! If your reader has to work to understand a paragraph, your point will suffer – as will your marks.

Let's take a look at the problems.

The first pronoun is 'it', halfway through the first sentence. Because it has followed several nouns – 'project management', 'field', 'area of expertise and research', 'the 1970s' – the reader has to *assume* 'it' refers to 'project management'. Again, hoping your reader assumes correctly is not ideal. Not only has the pronoun followed several nouns, it is many words away from the noun it refers to. This makes the problem worse.

Next, 'which', shortly afterwards in the sentence, is also problematic. The reader might think 'the eyes of the public' witnessed projects fail, which is reasonable. They might also wonder if 'the 1970s' witnessed projects fail – this is a more informal expression, and as such it is best avoided. Either way, the fact that 'which' does not *clearly* refer to a noun is a problem.

Then problems arise with 'these' at the start of the second sentence. 'These' projects seems to be the most reasonable (and correct) assumption, but because very soon more pronouns – 'this' and 'it' – appear that probably do *not* refer to the projects, the reader cannot be sure. This is another problem to note: if several pronouns appear close to each other, and refer to different things, your reader might be confused.

The pronoun 'this' which I've just mentioned ('this was compounded ...') does not seem to refer to a noun at all – unless the writer is using 'this' to refer to the 'standing' in the eyes of the public. However, this noun was so far back in the sentence, a reader has to go back and double-check what the writer means. Again, if your readers have to do this, your overarching argument will suffer badly.

Similarly, 'it' ('it was suffering from a poor reputation') might refer to 'project management' or 'the public sector'. In fact, the author means the 'public sector', and is attempting to demonstrate that, because the public sector already looked bad, high-profile failures within it were even more damaging. As such, here is a valid, clever point damaged by potential confusion in the reader.

The third sentence begins with another 'it'. The noun preceding it is 'reputation', which is fine. The lack of clarity around the previous 'it', however, might make the reader think twice about this assumption. As you can see, problems earlier in the paragraph are now damaging the reader's experience further on. Here, 'it' could refer to the very first noun, 'project management'.

In the final sentence, it is not clear whether 'some of them' refers to 'new methodologies' or 'positive news stories'. Use of the phrase 'some of them' presents the same problem – made worse by the fact that a new noun, 'organisations', has also been mentioned, adding a third option.

Below, I've adapted the paragraph. I have proceeded step-by-step, asking myself what each pronoun refers to, and making sure it is clear in the writing each time. Sometimes this has meant changing the order of words, repeating a noun or removing pronouns. I've also added a new noun ('damage') to make a pronoun more effective.

> ✓ Project management suffered in the 1970s, losing standing as a field and an area of expertise and research in the eyes of the public. The public witnessed several high-profile projects, mostly situated in the public sector, fail. This damage was compounded because at the time the public sector was already suffering from a poor reputation, which only began to improve after the introduction of new methodologies and more positive stories in the news. Some of these methodologies are still prominent today and organisations in the field work very hard to promote efficient project management; this promotion seems to be enjoying some success.

In some cases, above, I have added nouns to the paragraph. They are prefixed with a pronoun to demonstrate to the reader that I have control over the writing, and that I am deliberately linking ideas.

For example, 'damage' has not appeared until 'this damage' begins the third sentence. Because I use 'this', the reader knows I am referring back to something, and the noun 'damage' tells the reader I am describing the sequence of events in the earlier sentences as damaging. My point is made in an effective way.

Similarly, at the end of the paragraph, I write 'this promotion'. Earlier, the verb 'promote' was used. I link the noun to the verb with the pronoun 'this', and it becomes clear that I am shifting focus from 'the organisations' to the work that they are doing, with its results. In this manner, using a pronoun *and a verb*, where the verb has not actually been used already, can be very effective.

If a writer uses techniques in a *deliberate* way, the confidence shows in the writing, and the reader is more likely to follow an argument. In the first example, there was a sense that the writer did not have control over the paragraph, and that the reader had to make assumptions.

As well as leading to actual confusion, this lack of control can lead to the reader losing confidence in your writing. Confident writing leads to confident reading.

The final piece of advice on pronoun use is: make sure your pronouns agree with the nouns they replace.

This is often quite simple; in the following example, a masculine pronoun is used for a clearly feminine noun:

> ✗ Mother Teresa has suffered criticism, too. He has been attacked in several books.

That is at one end of the spectrum, and mistakes like that one should be identified during the proofreading process.

Here is another mistake, from an essay about the costs of healthcare; this mistake is slightly less obvious:

> ✗ A committee, made up of seventeen senior officials and ex-officials from the NHS, was established by the Minister for Health. The committee's report, after a lengthy editing process, was published in 2007. These suggested the financial state of the health system was deteriorating (DoH, 2007).

The final sentence begins with a confusing 'these', which is a plural pronoun. The most obvious noun this pronoun refers to is 'committee's report', which is singular. The reader, then, might think 'these' is referring to both 'the committee' *and* its 'report'.

While this is feasible, this is an example of how a grammatical mistake has forced the reader to question exactly what the author means – this is never a good thing.

Additionally, academic sentences should be *specific*. The author should make it very clear exactly where the suggestion has come from.

In conclusion: use pronouns sparingly but appropriately; ensure they agree with their respective nouns; make sure that your reader knows what these respective nouns are; finally, don't be afraid to combine pronouns with nouns where this will reinforce your point.

Articles

There are three 'articles' in English. This is relatively simple, compared to other languages. These three words fall into two categories. They are:

> ✓ Definite article: the
> ✓ Indefinite article: a, an

These words precede nouns. Note that there are many cases when *no article* is used.

49

Although the words themselves are short and simple, correct use of articles is quite difficult to explain. Even people who speak English every day use articles incorrectly when they write. The rules for using them are also difficult for people learning the language.

To give you an idea of how important articles are, here is a sentence with all the articles removed. It comes from an essay discussing complications associated with alcoholism:

> ✗ Problems arise due to phenomenon named after doctor who discovered it; Korsakof's condition leaves patient in dangerous situation with only slim range of treatments open to doctor caring for patient in hospital setting.

It is immediately apparent that articles play an important role in making sentences clearer. Instantly, the reader can tell that something is 'missing'.

The basic rules for deciding which article to use are given below. If you struggle with articles, I suggest finding a grammar book for people learning English as a foreign language.

'An' is used before words beginning with a vowel *sound*. 'A' is used before words beginning with a consonant *sound*. In most cases, this will simply be indicated by whatever letter a word begins with – but not always. So, use 'a study' but 'an investigation'; use 'a dissertation' but 'an in-depth dissertation'; use 'a European' but 'an hour-long European studies seminar'.

To determine which article to use, or whether no article is needed, ask the following questions of the noun. You'll notice that some answers end the sequence of questions, while in some cases you'll ask them all:

- Is the noun specific or non-specific?

    - A 'specific' noun will be one that a reader could identify in particular: perhaps it has been mentioned already; perhaps it is obvious from the context.
    - A 'non-specific' noun will not be specifically known to the reader. The noun might be being mentioned for the first time. Alternatively, the noun is a group, or general category, or a non-specific member of a general category.
    - Quite often, nouns move from non-specific to specific as the author mentions them once then continues to discuss them.
    - Specific: 'The'.

Non-specific: ask the next question:

- If non-specific, is the noun countable or uncountable?

    - To determine whether the noun is 'countable' or 'uncountable' try putting a number in front of it. Most common nouns are countable. Note that the issue at this point is not whether the noun is plural or not, just whether it *can* be counted. For example, you can write: three essays; two concepts; both elections.

- The following are examples of uncountable nouns: oxygen; sand; French; clothing; rice.
- Uncountable nouns tend to include: groups of similar items/some abstract ideas/ languages/areas of study/food.
- Uncountable: no article.

Countable: ask the next question:

- If non-specific and countable, is the noun singular or plural?

  - Singular: a/an.
  - Plural: no article.

Note that nouns being owned by another noun (the possessive case) do not take an article. You could not write:

✘ Toyota's the annual report …

but instead:

✓ Toyota's annual report …

or

✓ The annual report issued by Toyota …

In the last example above, the possessive is not being used.

To demonstrate these rules in action, here are a few more example sentences; note the articles used in each one:

✓ The studies conducted by Sorenson between 1980 and 1987 demonstrate her focus on bullying in a primary school.

✓ Primary schools can be sites of complex, unpredictable bullying behaviour (Sorenson, 1985).

In the above example, 'the studies' are specific in the first sentence, but only appear in referencing in the second. We are also told, in the first, that

51

Sorenson conducted her study in 'a primary school' – because this is being mentioned for the first time, the reader does not know it as a specific noun yet. If the school were mentioned afterwards, the definite article would be used.

In the second sentence, 'primary schools' is being used in the general sense, and is a plural, so no article is used. The same goes for 'sites'.

Here is another pair of sentences, comparing Marxism as a sociological perspective to its more political side; again, compare the article use in each:

✓ The consensus in more recent commentary (Harlin, 1986; Etienne, 1988; McMillan, 2002) makes this suggestion: as a critical perspective, Marxism has, arguably, performed more strongly than it has as a political ideology.

✓ Damage done to the ideological aspects of Marxism by historical events over the past 100 years has not had as much of an impact on its analytical power.

The first sentence mentions a specific 'consensus', easily identified by the reader because of the referenced research. 'Suggestion' does not take an article, but is preceded by 'this', which serves a similar purpose. Marxism is one critical perspective of many, and as such 'critical perspective' takes the indefinite article. The same logic applies to 'a political ideology'.

A noun begins the second sentence: 'damage' is used in the general sense, and is uncountable, so has no article. The specific nature of 'ideological aspects' makes the definite article necessary. 'Historical events' is a general group, countable and plural, so takes no article. '100 years' is specific, because the reader is explicitly told these years are the *last* 100; hence the definite article. The 'impact' is being mentioned for the first time, and as such is classed as non-specific. The 'analytical power' is being owned by the possessive 'its', so no article is used.

In both cases, 'Marxism' as a proper noun takes no article.

Modifiers (describing words and phrases)

'Modifiers' are words and phrases that provide a reader with more information or detail about parts of a sentence. They include adjectives and adverbs, which are describing words that have their own sections, below.

Some modifying phrases contain additional 'factual' information, or extra subject–verb–object arrangements. To show examples of this kind of modifier, that is not descriptive in a qualitative way, I've highlighted the modifying phrases in the next two sentences. The more descriptive modifiers are discussed afterwards.

✓ *Hamlet,* **written in various versions between 1600 and 1623**, seems to represent a shift in Shakespeare's tragic mood.

✓ **Although extensive research has been conducted on the disease in theory**, in practice, cancer remains a potentially traumatic and life-changing experience for any patient.

These modifiers are not the focus of this section. They are additional parts of a sentence, around the main subject–verb–object, that often appear, and often serve as a useful tool to vary our sentence structure. Descriptive modifiers are more of an issue.

I want to make a general point about descriptive language: academic writing does not, and should not, include extensive use of it. Remember that academic writing is objective. It is based on logic and reason: the writer uses evidence and gathers research to construct an argument that convinces readers of the writer's conclusion.

Descriptive writing is often more about *subjectivity*; how the writer sees something and chooses to describe it.

Key point

Some subjects studied at university do involve more subjective elements. I should know; I studied English and Creative Writing. Similarly, how can a Film Studies student analyse a film if they cannot use descriptive language?

Clearly, descriptive language does have a very important place in certain subjects. You are not likely to be describing artwork, for example, simply using adjectives and adverbs; you will be expected to go further than that.

There is a difference between the sentences in the first box, and the sentences in the second (all come from arts-based subjects):

✓ Shelley's later poems, including the two this essay focuses on, build on the themes of class struggle prevalent in the country at the time.

✓ Several critics (Hawthorne, 1979; Mitchum et al., 1987) have pointed out that twentieth century literature has produced two distinct visions of totalitarianism: Orwell's *1984* and Huxley's *Brave New World*.

(Continued)

(Continued)

✓ The film's opening shot, which pans slowly across an expanse of desert, immediately and effectively establishes the sense of isolation that grows stronger as the film continues.

✓ This prose poem was written after several attempts at writing a short story failed; the power of contemporary prose poetry, with a similar tone, is clear in works by Oakley (1999), Horley (2003) and Sukhvinder (2005).

✗ Most of the characters in the play are very realistic.

✗ The first half of the album is clearly more enjoyable and emotional because the lyrics seem to be more heartfelt.

✗ To reach the courtroom in the last episode's final scene, the two main characters must run very quickly.

✗ Every poem in this anthology has a wonderful rhyme scheme.

✗ It is a terrible shame that Walker died before he could write another novel.

Even though the sentences in the first box contain descriptive language, and – in almost all of them – the writer is making a point of their own about their subject, they are all appropriately written for an essay.

Points are supported, and none of the sentences in the first box involves the writer simply describing (using adjectives and/or adverbs) an artistic work in a subjective way, according to their views.

The second box *does* contain sentences that simply assign some descriptive language to a subject. Much of this description is subjective – 'enjoyable' and 'seem to be more heartfelt', for example. These sentences are not making a particular point but just describing artistic sources. No references are used in support.

Additionally, some of the sentences just narrate or provide basic information. Pointing out that characters 'must run very quickly', for example, is of no merit unless the importance of this is made clear. Simply describing events, whether they are in an artistic or fictional source or otherwise, does not often result in marks for your essay.

In fact, these points apply to any academic subject.

Remember: although you might be studying a subject that requires you to read and discuss artistic works, you are still expected to engage in thoughtful academic discussion and support your arguments with evidence.

Studying these subjects does not force you to reduce your writing to simple description of your reading, based on your own subjective opinions.

A general rule worth bearing in mind is – the *more* descriptive the modifier is, the more important it is to justify the description with references or by building up prior evidence. In a way, this is similar to emotive language; in fact, the more exaggerated a descriptive word or phrase is, the closer it gets to, potentially, being emotive.

To demonstrate what I mean by this, look at the following examples, all taken from an essay about the modern history of Afghanistan.

The first sentence is acceptable:

> ✓ The Taliban regime in Afghanistan was deemed by many official agencies, international organisations, historians and commentators to be authoritarian in nature (US State Department, 1997; Amnesty, 2000; Parker and Reynolds, 2003).

In the above example, the modifier (an adjective) is 'authoritarian', which is describing the noun 'Taliban regime'.

In the next example, however, a stronger adjective is used; an adjective so much stronger I think the author should spend more time justifying it:

> ✗ The Taliban regime in Afghanistan was deemed by many official agencies, international organisations, historians and commentators to be authoritarian (US State Department, 1997; Amnesty, 2000; Parker and Reynolds, 2003) and even medieval in nature (Johnson, 2002).

'Medieval' is quite a strong adjective in this context, and probably needs more justification than one indirect reference. In an improved example, I give more detail about the evidence that has led me to describe the subject of the sentence in this way:

> ✓ The Taliban regime in Afghanistan was deemed by many official agencies, international organisations, historians and commentators to be authoritarian in nature (US State Department, 1997; Amnesty, 2000; Parker and Reynolds, 2003). Some journalists went as far as dubbing the Taliban's rule as 'medieval' (Johnson, 2002: 97), basing this on specific practices such as stoning (Herbert, 2004).

Similarly, here is an example of a sentence in which quite a powerful adverb (the word 'rapidly', describing the verb 'shrinking') is given support and context with additional evidence:

> ✓ After his election, President Reagan signed Executive Orders that followed through on his campaign promises, rapidly shrinking the federal government: the pace of new regulations dropped to its lowest point since 1923 (Hollis, 1992) and government spending slowed by 8 per cent, compared with an increase of 14 per cent over the Carter years (Crelborne, 1998).

What I am demonstrating in this example is that *I*, as the author, have chosen to describe something as 'rapid', based on the research I have done (which I have then referenced). This is the aim in academic writing – to make it clear that you are formulating your own ideas and conclusions based on your studies. The sentence is a good example of this phenomenon, on a small scale.

Chapter 7 on conciseness and clarity discusses removing unnecessary description in more detail, but for now, note the following: words like 'very' and 'really', that can be attached to many describing words, add almost nothing to academic writing and should be avoided.

Adjectives

Adjectives are words that describe nouns.

Here are some adjectives; I've focused on examples more likely to appear in academic writing:

intelligent

well-founded

explicit

effective

detailed

important

rigorous

reflective

effective

In the box below are some complete sentences that contain adjectives:

> The case study explains that the company is **large**.
>
> Adjective = large
>
> Several **prominent** academics have published articles supporting this idea.
>
> Adjective = prominent

As the previous section explained, descriptive writing is not as common in academic writing as in other kinds of writing; when adjectives are used, they should be necessary and powerful.

Some adjectives do not 'describe' in the way we think of things being described – in the sentence I've written above after the example adjectives ('In the box below ...'), the word 'complete' is an adjective, describing the noun 'sentences'.

Effective adjective use

In addition to the general points made in the preceding 'modifiers' section, which covers both adjectives and adverbs, there is something else worth noting.

At certain points, other kinds of writing might have the description of something as the *focus*. When a new character in a novel is introduced, for example, sentences or even paragraphs might be devoted to describing this person.

Academic writing is different in that this kind of simple formulation – Noun + is + adjective(s) – even expressed in a more complex sentence, is very *rare*. Simply describing a noun is usually not an advanced enough way to be using your word count in an assignment.

This kind of sentence, for example, should not appear in your work:

> ✗ The sentences in Paulson's poem *Troubled* (1993) are all incomplete.

Rather, adjectives should be used to provide *key* information as part of the flow to make other points. If describing something *is* the focus of a sentence or paragraph, the description must be supported by evidence, and the importance of the description made clear.

In the following example, the adjectives give the reader important information while the author makes several points. The adjectives are describing things 'on the way', almost.

> ✓ The incomplete sentences in Paulson's poem *Troubled* (1993) contribute by their very nature to the sense of loss, as well as making the reader feel 'unusually uneasy' (Harkin, 2000).

You've just read another good example of the author's point of view (that the sentences, which are incomplete, work towards a theme in a poem) combined with a referenced source (the author links his own conclusion with a different but related point by Harkin).

In the next example, the description is the focus of the sentence, but the reason that it is the focus is clear:

> ✓ The sentences in Paulson's poem *Troubled* (1993) are all incomplete; none of the other poems in this collection employs a technique that is so immediately visible.

Although the description is the focus here, the author has explained to the reader that there is a reason for this.

Bearing in mind this rule and the rules described in the 'modifiers' section, two other important points concern adjectives:

- As always, make sure they are specific. Choose adjectives carefully.
- Unless you have a reason for doing so, you should not attach more than two adjectives to any noun in a sentence. As you've learned, most sentences in academic writing will have fewer adjectives than this, and many of them will be more 'informative' (as in the example I provided earlier, where the adjective was 'complete').

Adverbs

Adverbs are words that describe verbs. They commonly end in 'ly'. The list below shows some examples:

rapidly

commonly

explicitly

overtly

eagerly

Although I deliberately chose to provide examples of some adverbs more likely to appear in essays, generally, adverbs are rare in academic writing.

There are several reasons for, or factors behind, this rarity. For the same reasons that adjectives are relatively rare in essays, compared with other kinds of writing (again, the subject is an important factor here), adverbs are more so; description runs the risk of being subjective and not based in fact or on evidence.

Because verbs in academic writing tend to describe very specific, particular actions, the need to provide more description about how they take place should be reduced.

Removing unnecessary description is discussed in Chapter 7. For now, note that words ending in 'ly' benefit from extra investigation as you edit your work. Note that adverbs might most commonly be used in 'hedging', which is discussed in Chapter 3 (there are examples in the list below).

Effective adverb use

In addition to the guidance given in the 'modifiers' section, some additional points about adverbs are worth remembering.

Many adverbs that do appear appropriately in academic writing fit into four categories. I've listed the categories, and provided some examples of adverbs that you might consider using in each one. Adverbs that fall outside of these categories are more likely to be unnecessary.

- **Intensifying adverbs** – making a verb seem stronger, or have a larger effect
  - Examples: more; extremely; even; quite
- **Restricting adverbs** – narrowing the context of a verb
  - Examples: only; particularly
- **Hedging adverbs** – being careful so as not to jump to conclusions
  - Examples: usually; sometimes; generally; probably; relatively; perhaps
- **Additive adverbs** – signposting additional action
  - Examples: further; also

As you can see, most of the adverbs common in academic writing act as signposting language, pointing the way for the reader, rather than creating more subjective description.

Conjunctions

'Conjunctions' are small joining words. In a way, they are a very basic form of 'signposting language', which will be discussed in Chapter 4. Conjunctions indicate, in a simple way, the relationships between different ideas within a sentence or phrase. The most commonly used conjunctions are listed below:

and

but

or

so

yet

Other phrases that belong to a group of slightly different conjunctions include 'either ... or ...'; 'whether ... or ...' and 'just as ... so ...'.

Effective conjunction use

Sentences in essays and assignments should never begin with a conjunction (you might see this rule ignored in other kinds of writing).

Additionally, remember that conjunctions, like other words, have specific meanings and uses. Sometimes conjunctions are used incorrectly to stick unrelated sentences to each other in an awkward way.

Here is an example of this problem, which most commonly occurs with the word 'and':

> ✗ The company declared bankruptcy in 2002 and only one of the company's former executives continued to work in the field of biotechnology and his new venture became one of the sector's most notable success stories.

There are three grammatically complete sentences in the example. They are all linked only by the word 'and'. The word 'and' should be used to group related ideas, just as 'but' should be used to show that one idea excludes another, or that one idea is contrary to another.

If you find a complete sentence on either side of an 'and', you should probably just write the sentences separately.

The first 'and' in the example is unnecessary. The reader might get the impression that you are attaching ideas that come from the same topic together, rather than carefully thinking about how events, causes and consequences are actually related.

In this specific example, I think the second 'and' can remain, because the ideas are very closely linked; if the person in the example hadn't continued to work in a particular industry, his new company would not have been that industry's success story.

Prepositions

Prepositions indicate the position of, or sometimes the relationship between, nouns or pronouns.

Here is a list of the most common prepositions:

to

from

in

into

under

above

until

towards

between

beside

below

before

after

with

Effective preposition use

Ensure you use prepositions carefully. Think about the difference between these two phrases:

✓ The company put measures in place **before** the audit.

✓ The company put measures in place **after** the audit.

Both sentences are grammatically correct, but their meaning is very different, and will lead to different conclusions – just because of the different preposition.

Some verbs, or verb phrases, use specific prepositions – make sure you use the correct ones. For example, you 'focus *on*', 'tend *to*', 'withdraw *from*', and so on.

As you read and research in preparation for an assignment, look at the prepositions used and the phrases they are part of. Your vocabulary will develop and your use of them will improve.

Summing up

Familiarising yourself with the types of words most common in academic writing, in order to best make use of the 'effective use' sections in this chapter, is a valuable exercise. It is more immediately valuable than memorising grammatical terms without putting the concepts into practice.

In terms of the effective use of each type of word, the consistent advice is: use the most specific, meaningful words you can to make your point; vary your vocabulary where possible, but don't write strange sentences in order to do this; and finally, when in doubt about a particular word or phrase, remove it in favour of a simpler option.

The next chapter builds on this advice to clarify how these different concepts/terms are then used in sentences. Because the different types of punctuation are important in building up sentences, I discuss punctuation in the next chapter, and not this one.

Remember that some of the ideas and potential issues mentioned here appear again in later chapters (most likely the 'common mistakes' chapter), where specific aspects of them are discussed in more detail.

Further reading

Bourke, K. (2006) *Test it, Fix it: Grammar – Pre-intermediate.*Oxford: Oxford University Press.

- An excellent guide to key grammatical ideas, with plenty of examples, aimed primarily at those whose first language is not English, though it could be useful for anyone looking to brush up on their grammar. The examples are not necessarily academic in nature, but you should find you are able to apply what you learn here to your essay writing.

Bourke, K. (2006) *Test it, Fix it: Grammar – Intermediate.* Oxford: Oxford University Press.

- For those who have tackled the pre-intermediate entry in the series, listed above, this provides more of the same approach to fixing problems in your writing, at a more advanced next level.

Coffin, C. (2009) *Exploring English Grammar*. Oxford: Routledge.

- Rather than focusing on academic grammar specifically, this book examines the whole concept. It's probably slightly heavier-going than some of the other books on this list, but for those interested in the English language, it's a great read. Its discussion of the genre of text, in particular, as well as the nature of formality in writing, is excellent. The book contains activities, as well as excerpts from a wide range of real texts to highlight its points.

Crystal, D. (2004) *Rediscover Grammar*. Harlow: Longman.

- The focus here, again, is not necessarily on academic grammar. The book's sections on constructing sentences, as well as the clauses that make up sentences, are detailed yet readable. Topics like 'predeterminers' and 'relative clauses' highlight the level of detail this book goes into, far beyond the book you're currently reading.

Hewings, M. (2005) *Advanced Grammar in Use: A Self-study Reference and Practice Book for Advanced Students of English*. Cambridge: Cambridge University Press.

- As you might expect from the title, this is a comprehensive and more advanced book than some of the others I've mentioned. It covers tenses – including some I don't mention at all – particularly well, and also discusses 'clauses' – different parts of a sentence – in detail. The text is clearly organised and as such you might find it easy to dip in and out of; I'd probably suggest you don't try this in your first term, however!

3

Putting Sentences Together

Learning outcomes

By the end of this chapter you should:

- understand what a sentence is
- understand the key parts of a sentence, specifically the subject–verb–object arrangement
- understand the active and passive voices and the different effects they have on the reader
- understand what 'tense' is and the way it operates in sentences
- understand which tenses are most common in academic writing and why
- understand what is meant by the term 'hedging' and when it is appropriate in assignments
- understand the main elements of punctuation and how they are used; specifically, the full stop, the question mark, the exclamation mark, the comma, the colon, the semi-colon, parentheses (round brackets) and square brackets, the hyphen and the apostrophe.

Now that you're familiar with basic academic and grammatical conventions, the next step is to understand how to craft grammatically correct, effective sentences in your work.

Doing this builds on the rules this book has already discussed. As always, you should be aiming for simplicity and clarity.

The definition of 'sentence', provided below, is my own:

> A sentence is the smallest collection of words that makes grammatical sense and expresses a complete thought.

At the most basic technical level, remember that sentences begin with a capital letter and end with a full stop. Between that first word and the full stop at the end will be a variety of words and punctuation.

Key point

Sentence structure is also known as 'syntax' – you might see this mentioned in your feedback; it means the same thing.

There is no fixed rule around sentence length. Reading your work aloud is a good way of gauging whether your sentences are of an appropriate length: too many pauses and they are too short; running out of breath signals that they are too long.

As a rough rule, most sentences in academic writing are between thirteen and twenty words long (excluding citations; in the Harvard system I use, for example, these numbers would exclude the surnames in parentheses).

As your writing develops and you try to vary your sentence structure, making them different lengths is a good starting point. They should still end up somewhere between the numbers suggested above, however.

First, there is a basic grammatical arrangement your sentences should follow: subject–verb–object.

All complete, correct sentences will contain what is called a 'subject' (which will be a noun) and at least one verb. Almost all sentences in academic writing contain an 'object' (a noun). This basic grammatical concept is commonly called 'subject–verb–object' for the sake of simplicity.

Remember that this idea does not supersede or negate what you've learned about nouns and other kinds of word. These are new concepts that apply specifically to sentences; you can have a list of nouns on a page, for example, but a noun can only be the 'subject' of a sentence if it is performing a certain function in that sentence.

Subject–verb–object

All sentences have a *subject*. The subject will be a noun or a pronoun of some kind.

The subject is the part of the sentence that carries out the actions happening in a sentence. The subject is the noun that 'does' the verb.

As the previous chapter explained, a *verb* is an action word.

The *object* is the noun that is having the verb act upon it; it is being affected by the action of the verb.

Here are some simple examples:

✓ Eisenkopf writes novels noted for their use of language to parallel the mental states of their characters.

Noun = Eisenkopf

Verb = writes

Object = novels

✓ Although the theory has been criticised, the committee remains a recognised authority on the debate.

Noun = the committee

Verb = remains

Object = authority

✓ The increase in the use of learning management systems in further education has resulted in higher expectations among students making the transition to university level.

Noun = The increase in the use of learning management systems in further education

Verb = has resulted in

Object = higher expectations among students making the transition to university level

Key point

Some sentences, conceivably, could be grammatically complete with no object.

As you've been reminded, 'to be' is a verb. It is the verb in the following sentence; there is no object:

✗ This research paper is thoughtfully structured.

'This research paper' is the subject, 'to be' is the verb, and there is no object. 'Thoughtfully structured' is a modifier; it contains describing language, but no nouns.

Technically, this sentence is correct. However, as the 'modifiers' section in the previous chapter argued, this sentence is too simple for an essay. Academically appropriate sentences should not limit themselves to simply describing a noun, which is exactly what this sentence does. If a sentence has no object, it is probably doing something similar.

As such, always ensure your sentences contain an object.

As you write, edit and proofread your work, if you come across a sentence that seems incomplete somehow – this is especially noticeable if you read your assignment aloud – double-check the presence, and agreement, of a subject, verb and object.

Quite often, this sense of incompleteness comes from one (or more) of these elements being missing. It is important to remember that just identifying verbs in your sentence is not enough: verbs can appear as part of modifying phrases (in the box of three example sentences above, 'has been criticised' is a verb). Your sentences must have a verb carried out by a subject and affecting an object.

For example, the next two sentences are missing different parts of the subject–verb–object arrangement:

- ✗ In the literature, fierce debate around the role and achievements of grammar schools in the UK.

(Missing verb)

- ✗ By the time the advertising campaign had ended, increase in sales of over 23 per cent (Y.D. Industries Annual Report, 2007).

(Missing subject and missing verb)

Because the missing elements have been identified, it becomes easier to solve the problems:

- ✓ In the literature, fierce debate **continues** around the role and achievements of grammar schools in the UK.
- ✓ By the time the advertising campaign had ended, **the company had seen** an increase in sales of over 23 per cent (Y. D. Industries Annual Report, 2007).

You have seen, therefore, how understanding the subject–verb–object concept makes it easier for you to write complete sentences, and to rectify problems with incomplete ones.

Being comfortable with the concept also provides opportunities to vary your sentence structure. In the same way that you should vary your vocabulary where appropriate, you should write sentences that vary in structure.

However, you should not do this if changing sentence structure makes the sentence potentially confusing or hard to read; in these cases, it is better to stick to a simple structure that you are sure makes sense. Similarly, you should avoid spending too much time rephrasing sentences if you have other, more important issues to resolve in your work.

Varying sentence structure is a skill you will develop naturally as you write. That said, examining the subject–verb–object arrangement of your sentences is a good place to start learning. This way, you can identify areas where you can make simple changes to improve variation.

Going through one of your paragraphs, for example, you might find that your sentences break down like this:

> ✗ [Modifying phrase] + [subject] + [verb] + [object]. [Subject] + [verb] + [object]. [Modifying phrase] + [subject] + [verb] + [object]. [Subject] + [verb] + [object].

Clearly, this is quite repetitive. You might want to think about moving the modifying phrases around, provided you can ensure the sentences are still readable and grammatically correct. Combining this technique with varying sentence length, mentioned at the beginning of the chapter, can introduce considerable and effective variety into your writing.

Finally, understanding this subject–verb–object idea is crucial to grasp the concept of the 'active' and 'passive' voices in sentences.

Active and passive

Most sentences can either be written in the 'active' voice or the 'passive' voice. Basically, the different voices refer to the order in which components in a sentence appear. The phrase 'subject–verb–object' demonstrates the active voice. In a way, 'object–verb–subject' is the passive; although as you'll see, it is slightly more complex than that.

In reality, this choice only applies to some sentences. Some sentences, if swapped from active to passive, can be ridiculous; trying to switch certain passive sentences to the active can also result in some very strange writing!

The active voice consists of all or part of the sentence made up of the following formulation, which we've already seen:

> Subject + verb + object

The passive voice reverses this order. Because of this, the sentence has to be adapted slightly. The following examples will show why this must happen. Passive sentences almost always include a form of the verb 'to be' (often 'is' or 'was') and the word 'by'. Looking at some examples, you'll understand the reason for this.

> Object + appropriate form of 'to be' + verb + subject

Here, then, are two simple examples of the same, simple sentence expressed in the two voices:

✓ Active: The tutor delivers the lecture.
✓ Passive: The lecture is delivered by the tutor.

Here is another example with a slightly more complicated sentence:

✓ Active: President Clinton and a Republican Congress achieved a balanced federal budget in 1996.
✓ Passive: A balanced federal budget was achieved by President Clinton and a Republican Congress in 1996.

These sentences are complicated by several factors. Two nouns make up the subject; the adjectives 'balanced' and 'federal' are included with the object; and the modifying phrase 'in 1996' tells the reader when the action took place. In spite of this, the active and passive voices can still be used, and still result in the order of the same parts of the sentence changing.

The active and passive voices are both grammatically acceptable. Assuming you have a choice, then, which is better?

In *most* cases, the active voice is preferable. The subject–verb–object formulation is clear, logical, easy to read and, as the word 'active' suggests, gives a sense of the action moving forward in the sentence. The passive voice seems more deliberately formal, potentially old-fashioned and involves using additional words to make the sentence correct. If a sentence is already complex, the passive voice can make matters worse.

Only use the passive voice if you have a specific reason for doing so. Additionally, do not repeatedly write sentences in the passive voice, even if you have reasons for doing so – they will become very hard to read if used throughout a piece of work.

Use the trusty 'find' tool to look for the word 'by' in your assignments. If this highlights an example of the passive voice, revert to the active; unless you are using the passive for one of the following specific reasons.

Removing the subject of the sentence

The passive voice allows you, potentially, to remove the subject of the sentence. The most common reason for doing this is to avoid the first person – if 'I' is the subject. An example of this might look like the following:

> ✓ Active sentence: To reach the following conclusion, I analysed the results of various studies.
>
> ✓ Passive sentence: To reach the following conclusion, the results of various studies were analysed by me.
>
> ✓ Passive sentence with subject 'I/me' removed: To reach the following conclusion, the results of various studies were analysed.

You might also choose to remove the subject if you do not think the subject is important enough to be mentioned, or if the subject is likely to distract readers from the key point of the sentence. This choice will be yours as the writer; choosing to write in the passive and remove a potentially distracting subject is a specific technique available to you to make your writing more effective.

> ✓ Active sentence: McPherson-Daily published Anderson's seminal book in 1926.
>
> ✓ Passive sentence: Anderson's seminal book was published by McPherson-Daily in 1926.
>
> ✓ Passive sentence with subject 'McPherson-Daily' removed: Anderson's seminal book was published in 1926.

More rarely, you might not actually know what the specific subject of the sentence is; so you have to avoid using it.

> ✗ Active sentence: As a young man, the writer explains in his memoirs, [unknown subject] advised him to seek the help of renowned psychiatrist Dr Elsing.

> ✓ Passive sentence: As a young man, the writer explains in his memoirs, he was advised to seek the help of renowned psychiatrist Dr Elsing.

In the final example above, the active sentence is included for the sake of completeness and comparison with the other examples. The fact that it contains the '[unknown subject]' should make it obvious that this is not a sentence you would ever actually write. More important is the realisation that you have the passive voice available to you if you do find that you can't include the subject of the sentence.

Emphasising the object of the sentence

Choosing to use the passive voice because you want the focus or emphasis to be on the object of the sentence is, again, a decision you as a writer can make. Remember that the word 'subject' is simply a grammatical term; it's easy to get into the habit of thinking the subject of a sentence should be its most important part. This is not the case.

The following sentence, written in the active voice, is grammatically correct:

> ✓ Groups belonging to the so-called 'Christian Right' in America tend to dismiss the idea of global warming.

Just to clarify, the subject of the sentence is 'groups belonging to the so-called "Christian Right" in America'; the verb is 'tend to dismiss'; the object is 'the idea of global warming'.

In an essay discussing the various political beliefs or ideological activities of the group I've identified, this active sentence makes perfect sense. Because the subject of the sentence is the first thing the reader 'sees', there is the powerful impression that they are the focus of the sentence, carrying out various actions. The actions, the object and the additional information they add are of course very important (otherwise they would not be included at all), but it's clear what the sentence is 'about'.

What if my essay was about various aspects of the global warming debate? Or maybe my assignment discusses some problems that can hinder fund raising to raise awareness of climate change theory? Perhaps the actual group dismissing the theory is less a focus than the idea or debate around global warming itself. As a writer, you can make this decision, and decisions like this will subtly guide the reader through your argument. You can make your points more effective by ensuring the focus is where you want it to be.

If you did want to change this into a passive sentence, then, you'd write something like this:

> ✓ The idea of global warming tends to be dismissed by groups belonging to the so-called 'Christian Right' in America.

These decisions will be based on context: what you are writing about; the actual conclusion you are drawing your readers towards; where the focus of a particular part of your essay is, and so on. Read the two versions of the sentence again, and take note of the subtle difference. This difference would be made stronger in the context of a longer piece of work.

Varying your sentence structure

Although I have argued that in most cases the active voice can and should be used, if your sentences are all very similar, using the passive voice occasionally can help you vary their structure. This idea is summarised well by Jonathan:

> **WHAT YOUR TUTORS SAY**
>
> 'Vary the structure of your sentences in a paragraph. Don't always begin with the subject, especially if it's the same subject' – Jonathan, History lecturer

Be careful following this advice. It is better for your sentences to be clear and effective, if repetitive, as you are developing your academic writing. As your skills improve, you can use various techniques to vary sentence structure.

Tense

Every verb in your essays will be written in a certain 'tense'. As well as verbs agreeing with their subjects, which you read about in the last chapter, verb tenses must be consistent and correct over the course of sentences and paragraphs.

The tense of a verb signals to the reader *when* an action happens. Because all the verbs in a sentence will be written in a particular tense – often, but not always, the same tense – the reader will know whether the events described in that sentence happen in the present, happened in the past, began in the past but are still continuing, or will happen in the future.

Using different tenses is something you probably do without thinking in speech. If English is your second language, tenses can be a difficult topic, because different languages handle tense differently.

Additionally, many English verbs are known as 'irregular' verbs because they do not follow the usual rules when they change tense.

To give you a better idea of the concept of 'tense', Table 3.1 gives an example of the verb 'to write' conjugated in various tenses with the first person 'I'. 'Conjugating' a verb, remember, means making it agree with its subject. This kind of layout is very common in grammar books for learning languages.

TABLE 3.1

Infinitive:	To write
Simple present tense:	I write
Simple/imperfect past tense:	I wrote
Perfect past tense:	I have written
Present continuous tense:	I am writing
Future tense:	I will write

Because the first person, as we've discussed, is very rarely used in academic writing, Table 3.2 gives the same example, using the third person singular 'she' as the pronoun.

The English language does, more rarely, make use of more complex tenses. Just to give you an idea of what I mean, here are a couple more example phrases:

She will have written

She will be writing

TABLE 3.2

Simple present tense:	She writes
Simple/imperfect past tense:	She wrote
Perfect past tense:	She has written
Present continuous tense:	She is writing
Future tense:	She will write

A book devoted to helping someone learn English as a new language will go into detail about most of the different tenses. As well as the common present tense, English has the perfect past, the continuous, the future tense, the perfect future tense, the past historic, the conditional, and many more.

My aim in this book is slightly different, and I assume a basic knowledge of English. Because of this, I won't spend time going into this detail. Rather, I will focus on the key considerations you should be aware of when it comes to using tense in your essays.

The most common tenses in academic writing

Every time you write a verb, ask yourself the simple question: 'When is this action taking place?' If a sentence has several verbs in it, they will *often* be in the same tense, though I'll show you some examples where this is not the case. Similarly, then, most paragraphs will have a consistent tense running through them, unless there are deliberate changes in when the verbs happen.

I have provided answers to the question you should ask of each verb below. This covers the more common tenses.

- When does this verb take place?
  - The verb happens in the present: present tense
  - The verb is halfway through happening now: present continuous
  - The verb happened in the past, and the action is complete: simple past tense
  - The action will happen in the future: future tense

In Table 3.3 I then use a particular noun and verb to provide an example of the use of these tenses: 'Journalists' (third person plural) and 'investigate'.

The tense of your verbs should quite clearly reflect when something happens.

Tenses in a paragraph should only change when there is a specific reason for this change. Below I give an example of a sentence with several tenses being used within it.

TABLE 3.3

Present:	Journalists investigate
Present continuous:	Journalists are investigating
Simple past:	Journalists investigated
Future:	Journalists will investigate

✓ Because of the problems the corporation **has experienced** in the past, it now **operates** under a reformed management structure, **is conducting** a review of all its business processes, and **will implement** changes based on the recommendations of this review and others like it.

This sentence shifts from the past to the present. Then the verb 'is conducting' is written in the present continuous, because the corporation's review is ongoing. Finally, 'will implement' is an action that has not happened yet – it will take place in the future.

Key point

Although, as the previous example demonstrated, tenses will change – sometimes within a sentence – it is very rare for the most common tense in an essay to shift over the course of the essay. If you are *mostly* writing in the present tense in the first half of your essay, this should not shift to the past for the second half.

So if, for example, you are analysing a novel, and you decide to refer to characters, dialogue and themes in the present tense, make sure you stick to this approach throughout.

By simply asking oneself when a verb happens, you will shift tense only when necessary. Unfortunately, careless tense shifts do commonly appear in essays; you need to take care about this, as it can look lazy.

There is no reason, for example, for the tense switches in this example:

✗ Recent problems with rioting and in the UK **highlight** a general sense of discontent and dissolution. Although youth unemployment **could not fairly be blamed** for violent crime, young people still **worry** about a lack of solutions to their problems which the government **was not dealing** with. All parties that **are involved** in this **needed to work** together.

This is the most common kind of mistake with tense changing – a mixture of present and past tenses is being used. It seems that students more easily see the difference in the future tense, perhaps because it is used more rarely.

The problems in the example above would have been avoided if each verb had been examined and the question of when it takes or took place answered. At no point is a specific event that took place in the past mentioned. In the following box, I have corrected the example *and added a new phrase* that makes the past tense in 'could not fairly be blamed' appropriate.

> ✓ Recent problems with rioting and in the UK **highlight** a general sense of discontent and dissolution. Although youth unemployment **could not fairly be blamed** for the violent crimes that **took place** in 2011, young people still **worry** about a lack of solutions to their problems which the government **is not dealing** with. All parties that **are involved** in this **need to work** together.

In this corrected example, the present tense is appropriate throughout – except where I now mention violent crimes that explicitly took place in the past, in 2011. I inserted this to demonstrate, again, the power of asking when each verb happens.

Avoiding continuous tenses where possible

In the examples above, you've seen forms of the 'present continuous' tense. Continuous tenses are not confined to the present; the past continuous and future continuous are possibilities, too. A continuous tense is made up of the verb 'to be' in the appropriate form (the present, past or future tense) followed by the main verb ending in 'ing'.

Here are some examples:

> He is writing
>
> The lecturer was marking
>
> The group will be judging

Some languages do not actually have continuous tenses – just the simple present. The simple present tense is more direct, and because of this more effective in making a point. Continuous tenses in academic writing can *almost always* be replaced with the simplest version of the appropriate tense – whether that is past, present or future.

Below are some paired examples showing this replacement in some complete academic sentences.

✗ Members of the public sometimes forget that senior nurses are running complex bureaucratic institutions.

✓ Members of the public sometimes forget that senior nurses run complex bureaucratic institutions.

✗ Over the next five years, small business owners in America will be experiencing the effects of Obama's regulatory and tax policies.

✓ Over the next five years, small business owners in America will experience the effects of Obama's regulatory and tax policies.

✗ In this series of novels, the author seems to be suggesting that striving for wealth should not be criticised thoughtlessly.

✓ In this series of novels, the author seems to suggest that striving for wealth should not be criticised thoughtlessly.

In all these examples, a simpler tense can replace a continuous verb. Continuous verbs can be found by typing 'ing' into your word processor's 'find' tool. Although changing one sentence in the manner above might not make a huge difference, excessive use of continuous tenses is a strangely common problem. Changing several sentences in this way could really make your writing more effective.

Note that sometimes verbs that end in 'ing' are appropriate and correct. There are times when a sense of the continuous is needed; when you need to show the reader that something is or was *in the process* of taking place.

The following example of just such a case comes from a political essay, about the 2000 US Presidential campaign:

> ✓ Dick Cheney had been assigned to find a Vice Presidential candidate for George W. Bush and was conducting a search for one when Bush chose him for the post.

It's clear in this sentence that *as Cheney was carrying out his search*, he was chosen to be Bush's Vice Presidential candidate. If 'was conducting' was replaced with 'conducted', the reader would think that Cheney's search was complete before he was chosen. This provides a very different impression of the events.

To summarise – avoid continuous tenses, which are less effective and often unnecessary compared with simple tenses. If a continuous tense is used, there should be a specific reason for doing so.

Hedging

'Hedging' is a verb that refers to a technique quite common in academic writing – nothing to do with gardening!

It does not refer to one specific technique, but an idea. 'Hedging' can be carried out in various ways, but it can be summarised as a concept as follows:

Academic writing, by its very nature, is sometimes tentative. The writer must not jump to conclusions, or give the reader the idea that they are doing so. Academic writing often involves debate, different arguments and different conclusions. Writers must, then, accept that although they are engaging with the debate, and becoming involved in the 'academic arena', they might not have all the answers – or all the *right* answers.

'Hedging' refers to a broad range of ways in which a writer can show that they are being tentative: they are suggesting their conclusion *might* be the right one; that *it is likely* that they are using the broadest range of evidence they can.

By hedging, a writer is, at specific points in their writing, telling the reader: 'I'm not jumping to conclusions. I'm being careful, and honest, and tentative.' As such, it contributes to the honesty academic writing should possess.

Hedging when appropriate, and learning to do so in a variety of ways, is the mark of a good writer. In a way, hedging techniques are a kind of signposting language, because they contextualise a particular point to your reader, making clear that you are being cautious as a writer.

Let's take a look at some specific ways of hedging, with examples.

Hedging can often be done using certain verbs. Here are some common words that make clear a situation is not 100 per cent predictable or likely:

suggests

could

perhaps

seems

might

likely

potentially

possibly

Look at the difference between a sentence containing one of the above words, and a similar sentence that is not 'hedged':

✓ Results of the studies conducted by Olsen (1976) and Worthy (1984) make clear that this particular drug has risks if used in treatment over a long period.

✓ Results of the studies conducted by Olsen (1976) and Worthy (1984) suggest that this particular drug has risks if used in treatment over a long period.

Both show the author making a judgement on the strength of the evidence in their research; they are different judgements. It is more common in academic writing that you won't be able to make as strong a judgement as the one in the first sentence.

Sometimes, hedging can be done with phrases which clearly tell the reader that the author is being cautious. Another way of doing this is to acknowledge opposing or alternative arguments where appropriate, as in this example:

✓ Though others (Crichton, 1994; Benchley, 1998) have argued the opposite, this study shows that …

Ultimately, it is your choice when to hedge, and how cautious to be when you *do* hedge – here is a version of the second sentence above with another hedging word ('might') added:

✓ Results of the studies conducted by Olsen (1976) and Worthy (1984) suggest that this particular drug might have risks if used in treatment over a long period.

The point to remember here is that, if you feel you need to qualify a point, it is perfectly acceptable to do so using hedging language. In fact, careful and appropriate hedging is the mark of a confident writer. As usual, look for examples of this in your reading.

Punctuation

Punctuation appears in every sentence you write: understanding the most common parts of punctuation is vital. Because using punctuation is part of putting sentences together, I've included the topic in this chapter.

Here you'll find a short section on each of the *main* pieces of punctuation used in essays. Each section contains the ideas I think are most important to bear in mind when using that punctuation.

Be aware that some of the sections in a later chapter, 'Common mistakes', also discuss some issues specifically centred around the use of punctuation.

. The full stop

All grammatically complete sentences finish with a full stop. The only phrases or sentences that might not end this way would include bullet-pointed sentences, headings and other extraordinary examples.

Once you have written a grammatically complete sentence, put in a full stop. Then leave a space before you begin the next sentence. Full stops should never appear within a sentence, and are usually left out of titles, headings and subheadings.

Remember that a full stop acts as both a visual 'pause', and a similar break in a reader's head. The pause is not as long as that encountered when a new paragraph begins on a new line, but it is still significant. If you find yourself breathless when you read your work aloud, you need to break your writing down into smaller sentences – which will mean more full stops. There is nothing wrong with this.

? The question mark

Question marks end sentences that are framed as direct questions.

'Direct' questions almost always begin with a question word (like 'how', 'what', 'why', and so on).

As such, ending this example with a question mark is incorrect:

> ✗ The patient asked if this particular form of cancer was common in the United Kingdom?

Here, the sentence is one of narration; it is telling the reader that the patient asked a question, but it is not directly providing us with her question.

It is possible that this example could include a question word, but using a question mark would still be incorrect:

✗ The patient asked what the chances of survival for this type of cancer were?

Both these examples should take full stops, because the question is not being phrased as a question: read aloud both sentences after the word 'asked' and you'll realise the order of the words in the sentence mean these are statements.

If the direct question was provided through dialogue, using a question mark would be correct:

✓ The patient asked, 'What are the chances of survival for this type of cancer?'

Here, the order of the words 'what are' makes this a question. If you are ever confused about this, take the question from the sentence and read it aloud. Would you ask a question this way? Using the first example, read 'What the chances of survival for this type of cancer were'. This is not how you would ask the question (and it is not how the patient asked the question; the writer is merely describing the fact that a question was asked).

In the final example, the actual dialogue is being quoted, and it is phrased as a question would be asked.

However, dialogue will be rare in academic writing; certainly much rarer than in other kinds of writing. If you are studying something like English, you might well quote a lot of dialogue from the books you read. Other than that, however, most students will never write an essay with any direct dialogue in it.

This means that the only other circumstance that would involve the use of a question mark is the 'rhetorical question'. You may have heard this term before.

A rhetorical question is a technique, often used in speech, that is traditionally seen as a way of making the speaker's or writer's point seem more powerful. It is often described as a 'question not meant to be answered'. The idea is that a rhetorical question in, for example, a political speech, will make the audience think about the answer for themselves and understand the implications of the speech.

The following box contains an example from a (fictional) political speech, showing the most common way in which a rhetorical question is used. Note that this is *not intended to be an extract of academic writing*.

'Time and time again, we have been given the same excuses by this government; excuses for the poor jobs market, increasing crime rates and unclear foreign policy. Who will pay the price for these failed policies?'

The rhetorical question will probably not be answered (sometimes, the person asking the question will answer it themselves, however); the aim is for the audience to ask themselves the question, and then answer it – perhaps, in this case, with something like, 'Us?', 'Me?', 'My children?'

The rhetorical question is a powerful technique in writing or speaking aimed at convincing an audience to believe something. Given that an academic essay often has the aim of making a logical argument and encouraging readers to agree with its conclusion, it is understandable that students often ask if rhetorical questions can or should be used in academic writing.

The answer is – *usually*, no. Rhetorical questions should certainly not be used frequently. They can often tempt the writer to make emotive arguments, which you have already learned should be avoided.

The other problem with the technique is that, because academic writing should be transparent, open and honest, a question that is asked but not subsequently answered will make the reader worry that you do not know the details of your own arguments or points.

My general recommendation is to avoid rhetorical questions. If your writing does lead to a question that you want to point out to the reader, then include it and make sure you answer it. If it is phrased as a direct question, use a question mark.

These similar examples (one with a direct question, one without) would be acceptable:

✓ Given that the evidence overwhelmingly highlights the benefits of carefully planned and consultative occupational therapy programmes, a question arises: why does the government not do more to promote awareness of occupational therapy?

✓ The fact that the evidence overwhelmingly highlights the benefits of carefully planned and consultative occupational therapy programmes raises the question of why the government does not do more to promote awareness of occupational therapy.

As long as the writer answers, attempts to answer, provides some answers or even points out the difficulties in answering the question they have raised, then this is perfectly effective academic writing. Note that rather than being a question 'not meant to be answered' and designed to evoke a reaction in the reader, this is the writer clearly and openly pointing out that a certain specific question must be asked in the light of, presumably, what their essay has discussed up to this point.

! The exclamation mark

The exclamation mark should, as a rule, not appear in academic writing. This is unless you are directly quoting text that contains an exclamation mark. For example, if you are writing about a book or poem, and cite a passage from the text, include the punctuation as it is in the original. Beyond that, you'll almost never see this punctuation mark used in academic writing. Your word processor's 'find' tool, as always, can be helpful here. Just type '!' into the search bar. It is unlikely that you will have used this punctuation without being aware of it. Note that this is one of the academic conventions I don't follow in this book!

, The comma

The comma is a common, important and useful piece of punctuation. However, commas are often overused, and incorrectly used – especially in academic writing.

Chapter 8 on common mistakes contains more detail on this, but for now, I'll make this point: commas should not be used to separate grammatically complete sentences, but just to divide clauses. Don't make your sentences overlong by excessive comma use – most sentences shouldn't contain more than three commas, and this should not happen often: one or two is fine. If your sentences routinely contain three or more commas, think about breaking them down into smaller parts with full stops and some rewriting.

: The colon

The most common use for a colon is to signal the beginning of a list of words or phrases. The items in the list will be separated by commas or semi-colons, so the list will look something like this:

✓ The spread of 'globalisation' has consequences beyond the economic, affecting many other phenomena, including: terrorism, the spread of infectious disease, political upheaval and cultural identity.

The colon can also be used within sentences if the first part of the sentence poses a problem, or raises an issue, and then the second part of the sentence, after the colon, is a direct response to it. The colon should not be used for this purpose too often, but this is a good way of occasionally varying your sentence structure.

Here is an example of this kind of colon use, where the second part of the sentence is a direct 'reply' to the first part:

> ✓ More recent research (Collins, 2002; Kendall and Hepburn, 2007; Randall et al., 2007) has consistently highlighted a particular trend: homophobic bullying in schools is decreasing.

; The semi-colon

The semi-colon is slightly rarer than some of the other punctuation in this chapter. It is also harder to understand how to use effectively. Here I outline one of the simpler uses for the semi-colon, and provide an idea of another, more advanced way of using it. Note that if you are unsure, you can avoid the semi-colon entirely; there are always other ways of doing the same thing the semi-colon does.

The simplest use of the semi-colon is to separate items in a list, where the items are made up of more than one word. The items in the list might be whole phrases of varying length, and they might contain commas themselves. In a complex sentence that might already contain other commas, separating the list items with commas might confuse the reader.

Here is an example of such use. Note the colon, indicating the start of the list, and the phrases within the list, divided by semi-colons.

> ✓ The umbrella term 'Weapons of Mass Destruction' (WMD) refers to several distinct types of weaponry: nuclear weapons, also labelled 'strategic' WMD because of their capacity to inflict large-scale damage; biological weapons, also dubbed 'strategic'; radiological weapons, another category of 'strategic' WMD; and chemical weapons, which are often called 'tactical' WMD, because their capacity to cause damage beyond the battlefield, or over a wide area, is more limited.

Although the list itself is made up of only four items, the additional information about each item makes it necessary to clearly divide them.

Semi-colons can also be used to divide parts of sentences. Think of them as a 'pause' more substantial than a comma, but not as final as a full stop.

Elsewhere in the book I discuss the problem of 'comma splicing', where commas are used to separate grammatically complete sentences. You can use semi-colons to do this. If you have two complete sentences, and the second is so closely linked to the first that you think this link should be made clear, separate them with a semi-colon.

You can see an example of this in the box below:

> ✓ There seems to be a consensus that if election debates are to have more of an effect on the views of voters, real reform is needed; a new format is often mentioned as a potential starting point.

If you're in doubt about this, avoid semi-colons and just use two separate sentences. Additionally, don't try to use several semi-colons to separate several sentences: stick to two at most.

( ) Parentheses/round brackets

Some referencing styles make heavy use of parentheses – the Harvard and Vancouver styles in particular (see Chapter 6 on referencing). Other than that, they should not be used excessively. A rule of thumb is: if you remove the part of the sentence in parentheses, the sentence should still make sense – grammatically, and in terms of actual content. Parentheses can be used to provide additional information that is not *vital*, but potentially useful to your reader. Given that academic writing involves focusing on a series of specific, well-chosen points, you should not frequently be giving the reader 'extra' information. If you read part of a sentence that is in parentheses, and decide the information is very important, try using commas in place of the parentheses; or write a separate sentence that deals with the necessary content. Remember to add a full stop after, not before, the closing parenthesis.

[ ] Square brackets

Square brackets have a particular purpose as part of referencing. They're explained in more detail in the referencing chapter.

- The hyphen/dash

Although they usually look almost identical, the hyphen and the dash are, technically, two different pieces of punctuation. To keep things simple, however, note that both are usually considered too informal for academic writing. As such, they are best avoided. Note that this is a convention I ignore in this book. When hyphens are used in academic writing, they tend to appear *inside* words; they join certain types of nouns together, or add a 'prefix' to the start of a word to change its meaning.

' The apostrophe

The apostrophe has two main purposes: to replace missing letters in contractions and to indicate the 'possessive' – that is, to show that one noun owns another.

Contractions have been covered in an earlier chapter, but I'll recap the material here. Direct quoting is a part of referencing more generally, and is included in the referencing chapter. The possessive apostrophe is covered here. The apostrophe is often misused in all kinds of writing; this is unfortunate, because the rules are easy. Make the effort to learn them, and you shouldn't have any problems.

As discussed in the 'basic conventions' chapter, contractions consist of multiple words joined together and shortened by removing letters.

Here are some examples of contractions, as a brief reminder. The apostrophe indicates where the missing letters would be if the words were written out in full.

---

wouldn't = would not

she's = she is or she has (this should be clear from the rest of the sentence)

should've = should have

As the earlier chapter made clear, contractions should *not* be used in academic writing. They are very common in less formal kinds of writing and in speech.

In a way, this fact makes it easier to focus on the other roles of the apostrophe, because all the apostrophes in your assignments should be 'possessive' apostrophes, or used as part of referencing.

A 'possessive' apostrophe is used when you are making clear that someone or something (a noun) *owns* another thing (whether a concrete or abstract noun). The letter 's', known as the 'possessive s', is also used here.

The 'possessive s' is of course obvious in spoken English, because it can be heard. The apostrophe that goes with it, however, can't be heard; this means using it correctly is something only necessary in *writing*. Perhaps this is why it is often misused.

When one noun owns or possesses another, an apostrophe and the letter 's' are added to the end of the owner. If the owning noun already ends in 's' (this might be because it is plural, though this is not the only reason), the easiest option is to add an apostrophe alone to the end of the noun. (Some books and tutors might add an apostrophe as well as an additional 's'. Either option is correct, but I think that the double 's' looks confusing and is better avoided.) If there are several owners named separately, whether singular or plural, an apostrophe and letter 's' are added to the end of the *last named owner*.

Each of these cases is shown as an example below:

> The committee's report
>
> Dr Jones' report
>
> Jones, Ryan and Smith's recommendations

Let's look at some examples of the possessive in actual sentences.

> ✓ Robertson's theory, explained in detail in his article for the controversial September 2009 issue of *Modern Science*, has its admirers and critics.

The example contains several things worth noticing. The possessive 's', along with the apostrophe, has been used correctly in 'Robertson's theory'. Robertson, a person and as such a proper noun, owns a theory (an abstract noun). This is not a contraction; no letters are missing.

Key point

When you come across apostrophes in your work, it is easy to check whether you have used a contraction (which you'll need to remove) or a possessive (which you'll need to confirm is correct). Try replacing missing letters or words where you've used the apostrophe. In this example, I can't say, 'Robertson is theory, explained in detail …' or 'Robertson has theory, explained in detail …' As such I immediately conclude that this is a possessive – and that it is correct.

This is all relatively simple, which is why it is unfortunate when marks are lost through lack of attention to detail here.

The example goes on to mention something else that belongs to Robertson – 'his article'. The possessive apostrophe and letter 's' are *not* used with pronouns (as discussed, words that replace nouns). This is the same in speech. It would be incorrect to write:

> ✗ … in his' article for the …

When a pronoun is the owner in a possessive, do what I've done in the example; don't use an apostrophe:

> ✓ … in his article for the …

Here is another example, just to reinforce the point. Imagine that full example sentence was the second in a paragraph, and that Robertson and his theory had already been mentioned. This means we can use a pronoun for 'Robertson'. As such, the beginning of the sentence would change:

> ✓ During the last few years, a new way of conceptualising progress in biosciences, has evolved, originating in various works by Peter Robertson. His theory, explained in detail in his article for the controversial September 2009 issue of *Modern Science,* has its admirers and critics.

As you can see by comparing the two examples, possessive pronouns do not need apostrophes or the possessive 's'.

Finally, both examples contain one of the most problematic words I come across in assignments. The problem is an important and common one, but it doesn't need to be. That is why I'm going to make it a 'key point'! First, let's see what someone else has to say about this:

WHAT YOUR TUTORS SAY

'Its and it's always catch students out. The simple rule is not to abbreviate; then it is impossible to get it wrong. It's easy!' – Simon, Computing lecturer

I'm not as pessimistic as Simon – this issue doesn't 'always' catch students out. However, it does happen too often. Simon makes the same point I have made. If you are taking care to avoid contractions, you will never use the word 'it's'; if it does appear in your work, then it must be incorrect.

The fact that a tutor mentions this as a key grammatical concern shows that your tutors do expect you to have an understanding of grammar and to proof-read for 'small' mistakes carefully; and they see this mistake far too often!

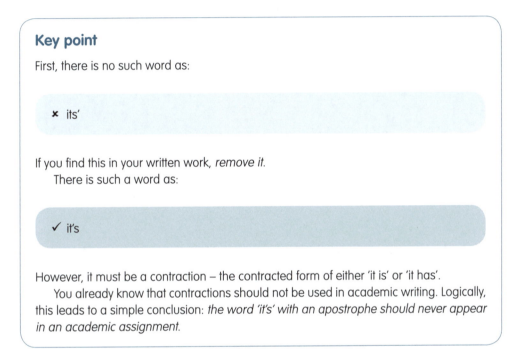

Key point

First, there is no such word as:

✗ its'

If you find this in your written work, *remove it*.
There is such a word as:

✓ it's

However, it must be a contraction – the contracted form of either 'it is' or 'it has'.
You already know that contractions should not be used in academic writing. Logically, this leads to a simple conclusion: *the word 'it's' with an apostrophe should never appear in an academic assignment.*

Key point

Sometimes a situation arises where you've used a word that is actually a singular word that *feels* like a plural, because it has several parts. For example, the word 'group' is a singular. If I was writing about the revisionists as a group, I would write, 'Most of this group's theories tend to oppose …'. When you are writing in a possessive context, think carefully about whether your noun is plural or singular. Think about the difference, for example, between 'staff' (singular) and 'members of staff' (plural).

Note that if a noun is a plural then you add an apostrophe and the possessive 's' at the end of the word. Two examples are 'the people's choice', if several people have made a choice, and 'the women's struggle for the right to vote'; in the second case, many women 'own' (or are part of) the fight for voting rights.

Further reading

Copus, J. (2009) *Brilliant Writing Tips for Students*. Basingstoke: Palgrave.

- Not only did I include this text as recommended reading for the first chapter, but I also list it here because its advice on sentence structure, punctuation and how to put sentences and paragraphs together is clear and excellent.

The 'further reading' section at the end of the next chapter includes books and other resources that you'll find useful when writing sentences, paragraphs and whole assignments.

4

Putting Paragraphs Together

Learning outcomes

By the end of this chapter you should:

- understand what is meant by 'paragraph'
- understand the range of purposes of 'signposting language', and have an awareness of examples of such language
- understand what a 'topic sentence' is and why it is an important part of a paragraph
- understand what makes an effective topic sentence, and what to avoid when writing topic sentences
- be able to conduct a simple numbering exercise to ensure each paragraph you've written deals with one main and specific topic
- be able to conduct a simple 'what, why, when' exercise to ensure each paragraph is serving a specific purpose.

Now that you have an idea of how to construct sentences, we will look to the next largest section of academic writing – the paragraph.

To begin, I'll provide a working definition of what a paragraph is.

A paragraph is a logically ordered sequence of grammatically complete sentences. This group of sentences expresses one idea or makes one point in considerable detail. All the sentences in a paragraph should contribute to this idea or point. They might potentially expand on it, but will not deviate from it.

Many of the principles behind putting sentences together also apply when forming paragraphs, which should be clear, simple and to the point.

It seems reasonable to assume that a paragraph made up of clear, well-written sentences will also be clear and well written. To an extent, this is true; provided you bear in mind the ideas discussed in the previous chapter, as well as other key ideas in this book (the referencing guidelines, for example), you'll find that your paragraphs are likely to be similarly effective.

There is more to constructing good academic paragraphs, however, than just writing decent sentence after decent sentence. This chapter will look at some of the ideas that make up the 'more' in this context.

In technical terms, the guidelines for laying out paragraphs on the page tend to be similar across subjects and institutions. They can only vary slightly.

Commonly, a new paragraph begins on a new line and is indented (which means that the first sentence begins further to the right than the normal page margin). Paragraphs that begin after a heading or subheading are the exception to this rule; they are not indented. Some tutors will ask that you also start each new paragraph with an extra space (that is, an empty line) before beginning the new paragraph.

Although this is probably the most that will be expected of you, it is always worth checking with your tutors or in your course handbook just to be sure. Also remember, of course, to make the appearance of your paragraphs consistent – if you are indenting them, and that's all you are doing, make sure you indent *every* paragraph!

Most academic paragraphs average between 45 and 75 words; going by the suggested figures for sentence length, given in the previous chapter, this means paragraphs will usually consist of between three and six well-developed sentences.

There will be many that fall outside this guideline, but if you are *consistently* writing shorter paragraphs, you should check that you are expressing your ideas fully enough; and if you are *consistently* writing paragraphs that are longer than this, take a look to make sure you are breaking your points down in a suitable way.

Paragraphs should discuss one particular topic, or make one point; the topic or point is then reinforced with the relevant detail, references, examples, and so on. Paragraphs should not address a wide array of subjects; nor should they make points that are too brief. I'll show you some examples over the next few pages.

You should be able to summarise a decent academic paragraph in *one* sentence (try doing this, informally, with friends). If you really struggle to do this, the paragraph probably needs some additional work.

While it depends on the assignment you've been asked to complete, and at what stage you are in the assignment, *most* academic paragraphs should contain a few well-chosen references. Effective referencing, including appropriately working our sources into our essays, is discussed in later chapters.

While individual sentences might be perfectly clear on their own, when you start to think at the paragraph level you should consider a powerful tool available to you: 'signposting' language. This is not a technical grammatical term, but is generally used to refer to a wide range of words and phrases that help the reader follow your argument.

I'll discuss signposting language in more detail later in the chapter; I mention it here because it is a good example of a technique that becomes more effective, and necessary, in paragraphs.

WHAT YOUR TUTORS SAY

'Attention to detail indicates that you care about how you present yourself' – Mariann, Biosciences tutor

Mariann's point is a very important one – she is suggesting that your tutors will be looking for effective practice in *all* aspects of your writing. An excellent essay written as one long paragraph (to take an extreme example) will betray the fact that the author has not paid attention to the detail of how paragraphs are arranged. This will undermine the whole piece of work.

Take Mariann's advice – use the opportunity of an assignment to present yourself well! This also brings me on to my next point ...

Key point

Sometimes students bring me essays that are excellent in many respects – *except for the paragraphing*. It is quite common for essays to not be divided into paragraphs at all, or divided a handful of times every few pages. More rarely, I see very short paragraphs that seem to start and finish randomly throughout the piece of work.

Sometimes, students don't seem to attach much importance to the idea of paragraphing correctly. Paragraphs, however, are vital (if they weren't, they wouldn't be in this book). First, they have a strong cosmetic impact on your reader, the first time they see your work – even if it's just a glance.

Like you, tutors marking your work will feel their hearts sink if they see pages and pages of text not divided into paragraphs at all. It means that well-written points can get 'lost' on the page, and their impact is reduced.

Writing that has been almost randomly divided up into very short paragraphs, or paragraphs that vary wildly in length, can lead your readers to think that you are being

(Continued)

(Continued)

lazy in breaking your work into its main points. Alternatively, they might wonder if you are not even fully aware of what your main points are. This is, clearly, not how you want your readers to react to your work!

Ultimately, paragraphs help your reader to see how you've arranged your points. They also help you ensure you've discussed a point in enough detail, and to assess whether you have presented enough of a counterargument. Paragraphs are as helpful a tool for a writer as they are a device for the reader.

Signposting language

A key technique that comes into its own in paragraphs is the use of 'signposting language'.

Signposting language is not an 'official' grammatical term. Additionally, it has quite a broad meaning. Signposting language refers to words and phrases that give your reader a sense of the direction your argument is going in. That is, these phrases 'signpost' the way.

While grammatically correct sentences and paragraphs can make effective points on their own, signposting language adds an extra level to an essay, providing the author with the chance to tell the reader various things.

Signposting language can say: this thing happened because of these other things; this idea opposes that one; these ideas reinforce each other; this idea is related but different; the essay's focus is shifting at this point; now the essay is going to highlight some opposing arguments; the essay is reaching its conclusion; all these things and many more. This might sound very complex, but when you see some examples, you'll realise that you use signposting language all the time, often without knowing it!

Before looking at specific examples of signposting language and what they are used for, compare the following two example extracts, from an assignment discussing the role of technology in education. They say similar things, but one is more effective than the other.

> ✗ The debate around the proper role of online learning remains highly charged, despite massive advances in the technology that can be involved in it. Beyond the often emotional nature of a debate so close to the hearts of academics, many conclusions are apparent in the research. Parker (2003), Maxwell and Roberts (2006) and JISC (2010) maintain that the benefits of 'well-deployed' technology-enhanced learning (Maxwell and Roberts, 2006: 307) can be exponential.

Meyer (2005) and Holmes (2008) argue that more traditional forms of teaching are still highly valued. A wide range of research (Jackson, 2004; Wyle, 2006; Tomlin, 2007) reaches conclusions somewhere in between. Over the years, students themselves have become increasingly vocal (NUS, 2011) in demanding what Meyer disparages as 'the best of both worlds' (2005: 198). It seems that involving oneself in this discussion involves careful dissection of the arguments.

✓ The debate around the proper role of online learning remains highly charged, despite massive advances in the technology that can be involved in it. Beyond the often emotional nature of a debate so close to the hearts of academics, **however**, many conclusions are apparent in the research. **On the one hand**, Parker (2003), Maxwell and Roberts (2006) and JISC (2010) maintain that the benefits of 'well-deployed' technology-enhanced learning (Maxwell and Roberts, 2006: 307) can be exponential.

On the other hand, Meyer (2005) and Holmes (2008) make the **contrasting** argument that more traditional forms of teaching are still highly valued. **Alternatively**, a wide range of research (Jackson, 2004; Wyle, 2006; Tomlin, 2007) reaches conclusions somewhere in between. Over the years, **additionally**, students themselves have become increasingly vocal (NUS, 2011) in demanding what Meyer disparages as 'the best of both worlds' (2005: 198). It seems, **then**, that involving oneself in this discussion involves careful dissection of the arguments.

The addition of a few well-chosen phrases (highlighted in bold) makes the writing more effective. Each instance of signposting language in the second version of the extract has a specific meaning, and is being used carefully. As with any other word or phrase, signposting language should be used in a precise and appropriate way.

Look back over the paragraphs in this book, and you'll see that I regularly use signposting language. Without these words and phrases, academic writing would be a series of statements. The reader would be forced to construct links between these statements themselves. Remember that effective academic writing creates a logical argument; a progression of points building to a conclusion. In doing so, academic writing does not rely on the reader creating this progression themselves; signposting language helps the reader follow this progression more closely.

Signposting language can be used to highlight the relationship between specific points, as it does in this example, from an essay discussing the 2004 US Presidential election:

> ✓ Some analysts blame Kerry's loss on the tendency of his campaign to focus on biography (Underwood, 2005; Johnson, 2006). **Alternatively**, a different school of thought suggests that important social issues on the ballot in several states drove up the number of Republican voters (Ryan, 2007).

In the above example, the word 'alternatively' makes it clear that a *different reason* for the *same outcome* is being proposed.

Additionally, signposting language can signal to the reader where the essay itself is going, as it does in this example from later in the same politics essay:

> ✓ The range of arguments explaining the outcome of the 2004 election and the lack of *overwhelming* evidence for any one suggest, **in conclusion**, that John Kerry suffered defeat because of a multitude of reasons.

The key to effective signposting is to do so very specifically. Don't just sprinkle these words and phrases through a piece of work as you proofread; make sure you think through how to use them appropriately as you write.

Below are some of the most common phrases, as well as the context in which you'd use each one.

Presenting contrasting ideas/arguments

by contrast

in contrast to

however

on one hand/on the other hand

rather

conversely

in comparison

compared to

Providing different reasons/evidence that have the same result or making a similar point

alternatively

likewise

again

---

also

additionally

similarly

equally

in addition

Setting up a conclusion

in conclusion

finally

overall

lastly

Summarising evidence

to summarise

in summary

overall

Demonstrating cause and effect

because of

despite

Providing examples

for example

for instance

namely

such as

Emphasising a point

indeed

in fact

furthermore

moreover

(Continued)

97

(Continued)

Being more specific

in particular

in relation to

in terms of

more specifically

particularly

In addition to the above phrases, it is worth bearing in mind that almost any sentence or part of a sentence can act as a 'signpost', by creating direction for the reader.

In the following extract (from an essay discussing a director's filmography), for example, a different kind of phrase is used:

✓ Rogers has said in various interviews (*Time*, 1980; *Newsweek*, 1985) that his films tend to reflect his political views overtly and explicitly. **These statements give the audience an idea of how to interpret his most recent work, *Exodus*.**

The phrase in bold is essentially telling the reader that what will follow are the various ideas involved in interpreting a particular film.

In this way, as you write paragraphs, you will use the common signposting phrases mentioned above; it is also, however, worth thinking about how other phrases can prepare the reader for the progression of your argument. If you need to tell the reader what is coming next, do so.

Topic sentences and staying on topic

Almost every paragraph of good academic writing in an assignment will contain a 'topic sentence'. In fact, the first sentence in a paragraph is often the topic sentence. It's certainly easiest, when getting started writing essays, to write them at the beginning of your paragraph (you can always, if appropriate, move them around later). Topic sentences can also finish a paragraph. Less commonly, you can find a topic sentence somewhere in the middle of a paragraph.

So what are topic sentences? The clue is in the name. Read the following example paragraph, from an essay about the Mormon religion:

✓ Mormonism continues to have a rapidly developing, evolving public profile. The religion is not only growing in numbers of followers (Fyne, 2010), but is sometimes hotly debated in the American media. Recent popular books (Krakauer, 2006; Jefferies, 2009) have presented both criticism and investigation into Mormons, particularly in the USA. Additionally, high-profile adherents have been advancing through the political arena in recent years, notably Democratic Senator Harry Reid and Republican Governor Mitt Romney, twice a presidential candidate.

One sentence in this example acts as a kind of summary of the others. If not a summary, it certainly identifies the main theme or idea the paragraph is discussing.

I gave you a hint in the beginning of this subsection – it's the first sentence. The other sentences are all grammatically correct, and could stand alone. Imagine the paragraph without that first sentence – it would just be a series of factual statements. With this topic sentence, the writer has made a clear, strong point (about the increasing public awareness of Mormonism) and then reinforced it with other sentences that provide a range of appropriate evidence.

Topic sentences usually either act as summaries, or point out a key theme or idea. They can work in different ways, depending on the nature of the paragraph. In that first example, we had a topic sentence making a point, and the other sentences providing the evidence that, in the writer's view, proves that point.

In this next example, from an essay on scientific research, the topic sentence is doing something slightly different:

✓ Early in his first term, President Bush issued a controversial ruling about stem cell research (Mack, 2004). The debate about climate change continues, and several scandals have rocked the consensus in recent years. The long-term effects of a serious oil spill will make themselves clear over time after the BP spill off the gulf coast. Awareness of the potential moral dangers associated with the intertwining of bioethics, nanotechnology and similar fields, have moved from otherworldly science fiction into serious discussion (Mukherjhee, 2008). Clearly, science as a broad field is still filled with vigorous, potentially emotional debate, and the future contains serious challenges that science both poses and hopes to address.

Here, the topic sentence is the last one. Again, the others provide the *detail* and consist of effectively written, linked facts. It is the topic sentence that explicitly makes the link. The other sentences are *examples* of the main idea in the topic sentence: that debate and challenges exist in contemporary science.

The writer has skilfully picked varied examples, so the other sentences are equally important – but it is in the last sentence that the writer's own strength in grouping these examples shows. Note the signposting language: after all of these examples, the writer is confident enough to say to the reader, 'clearly ...', which works more subtly, perhaps, than a more obvious alternative – for instance, a phrase like 'these examples prove that ...', which would also perform a similar purpose.

It is worth taking a look at one more example of a topic sentence before I summarise their potential purposes and importance. This paragraph is from an essay about a British poem:

> ✓ Although the theme has clearly been established in the first stanza of the poem, the second stanza really develops the theme of growing distance between the aristo-cratic and poorer classes in England. This can clearly be seen in the phrase ...

Here, you can see a strong topic sentence that is clearly identifying the writer's next focus: the *second* stanza (verse) of a poem. The signposting word 'although', and the rest of the first phrase, also make a distinction between the ideas in previous paragraphs, and the ideas to come in the following sections.

An effective topic sentence is *not* a brief statement of fact – you as a writer should be demonstrating some way of engaging with the topic. The topic sentence above, from the essay analysing a poem, is a good example of this.

Topic sentences should *not* be brief value judgements that are not backed up with evidence in some way (simply labelling something associated with the topic/subject 'good' or 'bad'). Topic sentences should also be very specific and about some particular aspect of the topic.

Poor topic sentences often make it harder for you to know how to develop the rest of your paragraphs.

Below are some examples of the kinds of sentences that would make very poor topic sentences. Beyond that, these sentences would be ineffective wherever they appeared in an assignment.

> ✗ The band's most groundbreaking album was released in 1982.
>
> ✗ George Galloway belonged to the Labour Party before he left to form Respect, the party he represented in Parliament until 2015.
>
> ✗ The effects of climate change are terrible.

These examples could quite easily come from more journalistic or popular writing. The first two are just statements of fact. The writer is not setting up an interesting paragraph. Try to make it obvious that you as the writer are present in your topic sentences. By this I mean that your topic sentences are a great opportunity to present the critical details that form your argument.

The third example seems dangerously subjective and far too brief for an academic point. To say something, particularly a broad and complex theory like climate change, is 'bad' (or 'good') without justification or detail is not academically appropriate. This topic sentence does not provide such justification *or*, crucially, introduce it.

It is true that the rest of the paragraph that this topic sentence comes from might include examples of the effects of climate change. However, this would result in a paragraph made up of a weak, subjective value judgement, followed by simple factual statements. These statements might be referenced, but this would still be descriptive writing, not academically engaged writing.

The chapters on critical thinking and referencing provide more information on this. For now, be aware that the focus of academic writing is not on facts.

If anyone could look at an encyclopedia, news report or internet post, and find versions of your topic sentences, or all the facts within them (the sentence about George Galloway above is a perfect example of this), you have a problem. Your topic sentences are too descriptive and factual.

Instead, topic sentences should do something more. They should prove to the reader how you are engaging with a topic and reaching your own conclusions *based on your research.*

Here are some stronger topic sentences, on the same topics:

> ✓ At the time, critics saw the band's 1982 album as a failure, though the fact that it is seen more positively now highlights the band's presaging a shift in attitudes to music.
>
> ✓ George Galloway's departure from the Labour Party can be seen as a move that highlighted his own political shift, or the Labour Party's; perhaps both.
>
> ✓ While climate change, broadly, has had many effects on the world, some positive and many damaging, some key consequences can be identified by examining the effects and their differences across continents.

If you've written a poor topic sentence, the best remedy is probably re-examining the entire paragraph, rather than simply replacing the sentence with a better one. That said, you might find, on examining the paragraph, that this is all that's necessary. I'm simply suggesting it's best not to *assume* this simple replacement is the solution.

The point I am making is that your assignment briefs should provide plenty of scope to build an effective, logical argument based on your engagement with your research material. This is more than simply reciting facts.

As such, think about the main point you want to make in a paragraph. Put that specific point into a topic sentence in a way that will also allow you to develop or add more detail in the following sentences. The revised examples offer a much better opportunity to include references in a way that proves that the writer has actually engaged with their reading, not just learned facts about a certain topic.

Sometimes, topic sentences will include signposting language, or act as signposts themselves. For example, if I've written a paragraph explaining how climate change has affected developing countries comparatively more negatively than other countries, I might write this topic sentence at the start of the following paragraph:

> ✓ However, some of the effects of climate change, and the climate change debate, could be seen as affecting the developing world in a more *beneficial way*.

Again, by making it clear that I will be presenting a different group of examples from my research, this topic sentence is demonstrating that I have engaged with what I have read.

This next example, from an English essay, is also acting as a kind of signpost. Here, the writer is moving on from discussing a novel, to focusing on a compilation of short stories – both by the same author.

> ✓ By contrast, the post-colonial themes so strongly established in all of Willis' novels up to this point, do not seem to provide the same undercurrent in the collection of short stories.

Both examples contain some of the signposting phrases I've mentioned elsewhere in the chapter. They also, as good topic sentences, make a clear and specific point that provides plenty of potential to go into more detail and develop the point.

Trying to identify the topic sentences in the paragraphs you read, and developing the skills to write them effectively, are valuable exercises. Writing good topic sentences will also have a positive impact on your paragraphs as a whole. This is because an effective topic sentence tends to push an author towards more thoughtful, detailed and engaging paragraphs.